PATONS &
BALDWINS'
HELPS TO
KNITTERS
2/557

PATONS &
BALDWINS'

PRICE
2D.

MAN'S PULL-OVER
FROM PATON'S SUPER OR BEEHIVE FINGERING

🐝 **Patons**

JILL JAGO · JACQUE EVANS

KNITTING NOSTALGIA

KNITWEAR 1920-1950
Today's Styles from Yesterday's Designs

Photographs by
Jill Furmanovsky

VIKING

VIKING
Penguin Books Ltd, Harmondsworth, Middlesex, England
Viking Penguin Inc., 40 West 23rd Street, New York, New York 10010, U.S.A.
Penguin Books Australia Ltd, Ringwood, Victoria, Australia
Penguin Books Canada Ltd, 2801 John Street, Markham, Ontario, Canada L3R 1B4
Penguin Books (N.Z.) Ltd, 182–190 Wairau Road, Auckland 10, New Zealand

First published 1985

Type set in Photina

Printed in Great Britain by Butler & Tanner Ltd, Frome and London

British Library Cataloguing in Publication Data
Jago, Jill
    Knitting nostalgia: knitwear 1920–1950.
    1. Knitting—Patterns
    I. Title   II. Evans, Jacque
    746.43'2041   TT820
    46/2015
ISBN 0-670-80879-2

LCCCN; 85-51382

To our mothers, Freda Nicholls and Lilian Evans,
who taught us to knit in the first place

Acknowledgements

Thanks to everyone who helped, researched and
generally supported us.

Special thanks to:
Sally Gaminara at Penguin Books for her help and
determination.
Everyone at Patons – in Alloa, Darlington and
London.
Especially – Nan Govan in Alloa, for her patience and
valued help; John Morgans in Darlington, for
initiating the project; Ron Irons, also at Darlington,
for agreeing to help; Sandra Cook in London, with
Joan Proudfoot, for undertaking the immense task of
transcribing the patterns; Rose Munir for dispatching
yarns and advice to our knitters all over England.

Frances Hinchcliffe at the Textile Department of the
Victoria and Albert Museum, Brompton Road,
London.

Personal thanks to:
Melvin Yates for much support, including days locked
in the dark room processing film; Lesley Evans for
helping to choose the patterns in Scotland; Roger
Jago for modelling free of charge and acting as
messenger; Rosanna Greenstreet for all the general
help; Nick Houghton and Douglas Druce for
information about the periods.

Special thanks to our knitters; Joan George, Mrs
Garthwaite, Dawn Law, Marjory Pointer, Sally Morse,
Eva Barber, Mary Davies, Frances Edwards, Lilian
Evans, Liz Marriott, Nancy Boud, Jane Griffiths, Ruth
Bibby, Doris Baker, Jo Grant, Gladys Broom, Liz
Abbott, Kate Butcher and Patricia Boyden.

Contents

Introduction

If it hadn't been for a P&B twopenny leaflet, *circa* 1920, that Jacque Evans picked up in a south London jumble sale, the patterns in this book might well have remained for ever in Patons archives in Alloa, Scotland.

Jacque asked John Morgans at Patons to update her pattern and when the result was knitted, the idea for the book was born. Off we went to the historic Patons factory near Stirling; and with Nan Govan's immense patience and good humour, we unearthed a treasure trove of nostalgia, romance – and above all, sheer style; the patterns in this collection represent a mere fraction of the many hundreds – quite apart from wildly appealing but totally impractical bathing dresses and other thoroughly crazy outfits – that we had to leave for another time.

The items range from easy to knit to frankly pretty difficult; but as neither of us are very experienced knitters we selected as far as possible those patterns that we felt most confident about knitting ourselves; as well as producing the book we also produced an item each for inclusion!

Sandra Cook at Patons, assisted by Joan Proudfoot, transcribed all the patterns for modern yarns and needles; and as far as possible replaced the original 2, 3 and 4 ply yarns (popular in the more leisurely early years of this century, but not today) with thicker alternatives. Sandra and Joan also completely redesigned many of the patterns, and in a sense modernized them to suit today's rather different proportions.

A few treasures positively refused resuscitation and sadly, had to be left in peace! But we think we finally got the mix right between the delightful eccentricity of the period – accessories, mad hats and quirky geometric shapes – and its classic style.

The mens' lot is at least as appealing as the women's – shades of Basil Rathbone and Douglas Fairbanks lurk in the distinctive cable and patterned pullovers of the era, now favoured by a new generation of fashionable young men.

For many readers the book will undoubtedly unlock many memories. I remember the day war broke out – though not very clearly. Jacque almost remembers the day it ended, so both of us have, in our time, worn garments very similar to many of these. Now we will be wearing them again – just for the fun of it!

So, for hand-knitters everywhere, here's a small part of the immense pleasure we've had in putting this book together.

Special Notes

The instructions for the designs in this book have been transcribed from original patterns issued by Patons and Baldwins between the years 1920 and 1950. The approximate dates of origin are shown with each pattern. In some cases there are slight differences between the original and the updated versions. Some of the original designs were knitted in fine 2 and 3 ply yarns which are now largely unavailable and certainly unfashionable, so additional modifications have been made to these particular designs to make them more practical to knit and to wear.

It is impossible to describe patterns as 'easy' or 'difficult', because different knitters will have different ideas about these descriptions. It is therefore advisable to read patterns through very carefully before starting.

Tension
Successful results can be achieved only with accurate tension. Check your tension, using the yarn and needles specified in the pattern, by knitting a 10 cm square in the stitch described in the note on tension given with each pattern. Measure and compare the number of stitches and rows with the correct tension. If you have more rows and stitches than you should, repeat the sample with a larger size needle – if you have less, try a smaller size.

Note
This is even more vital when selecting an alternative yarn to that specified in the pattern.

Alma
Woman's Lace-panelled Cross-front Sweater (1924)

Mid-twenties elegance for evening or for afternoon cocktails – or perhaps a tea dance. Definitely not for beginners, but the lovely Clara Bow effect is worth the extra effort.

To fit bust		cm	86	91	97
(approx)	in	34	36	38
Approximate length from top of shoulders		cm	66	67	68
	in	26½	26½	27
Sleeve seam		cm	14	14	14
(approx)	in	5½	5½	5½
Patons Beehive (knits as 4 ply)	50 g balls		9	9	10

Pair each Nos. 2¾ mm and 3¼ mm needles.
5 buttons.
Length of narrow elastic.

Tension
On No. 3¼ mm needles, 28 sts and 36 rows to 10 cm (stocking stitch).

Abbreviations
K = knit; P = purl; st = stitches; tog = together; sl1 = slip 1 stitch knitways; psso = pass slip stitch over; yfwd = yarn forward; dec = decrease; patt = pattern; rep = repeat; cm = centimetres; in = inches; mm = millimetres.

RIGHT FRONT
With No. 3¼ mm needles, cast on 91 [95,99] sts and work in patt as follows:
1st row (right side) – (K1, P1) 3 times, K1, *(yfwd, sl1, K2 tog, psso, yfwd, K1) 3 times, K9 [10,11]; rep from * to end.
2nd row – P to last 6 sts, (P1, K1) 3 times.
3rd row – (K1, P1) 3 times, K to end.
4th row – As 2nd.
These 4 rows form patt.
Continue in patt until Front measures approx 24 cm, ending with 4th row of patt.
Next row – Patt to end, cast on 39 [40,41] sts for sleeve. *130 [135,140] sts.*
1st row – (K1, P1) 3 times, P to last 6 sts, (P1, K1) 3 times.

2nd row – (K1, P1) 3 times, K to last 6 sts, (P1, K1) 3 times.
3rd row – As 1st.
4th row – (K1, P1) 3 times, K1, *(yfwd, sl1, K2 tog, psso, yfwd, K1) 3 times, K9 [10,11]; rep from * to last 18 sts, (yfwd, sl1, K2 tog, psso, yfwd, K1) 3 times, (P1, K1) 3 times.
Continue in patt until work measures 23 [24,25] cm from cast-on sleeve sts, and end with right side facing for next row.
Next row – (K1, P1) 3 times, K1, (K4 tog) 11 times, K0 [2,3] tog, patt to end. *97 [101,105] sts.*
Cast off.

LEFT FRONT
With No. 3¼ mm needles, cast on 91 [95,99] sts and work in patt as follows.
1st row (right side) – K1, *K9 [10,11], (yfwd, sl1, K2 tog, psso, yfwd, K1) 3 times; rep from * to last 6 sts, (P1, K1) 3 times.
2nd row – (K1, P1) 3 times, P to end.
3rd row – K to last 6 sts, (P1, K1) 3 times.
4th row – As 2nd.
These 4 rows form patt.
Continue in patt until Front measures approx 24 cm, ending with 3rd row of patt.
Next row – Patt to end, cast on 39 [40,41] sts for sleeve. *130 [135,140] sts.*
1st row – (K1, P1) 3 times, K1, (yfwd, sl1, K2 tog, psso, yfwd, K1) 3 times, *K9 [10,11], (yfwd, sl1, K2 tog, psso, yfwd, K1) 3 times; rep from * to last 6 sts (P1, K1) 3 times.

2nd row – (K1, P1) 3 times, P to last 6 sts, (P1, K1) 3 times.
3rd row – (K1, P1) 3 times, K to last 6 sts (P1, K1) 3 times.
4th row – As 2nd.
Continue in patt until work measures 23 [24,25] cm from cast-on sleeve sts, ending with right side facing for next row.
Next row – Patt to last 51 [53,54] sts, K0 [2,3] tog, (K4 tog) 11 times, K1, (P1, K1) 3 times. *97 [101,105] sts.*
Cast off.

BACK

With No. 3¼ mm needles, cast on 144 [151, 158] sts and work in patt as follows.
1st row (right side) – K1, *K9 [10, 11], (yfwd, sl1, K2 tog, psso, yfwd, K1) 3 times*; rep from * to * twice more, K8, rep from * to * 3 times more, K9 [10, 11].
2nd row – P.
3rd row – K.
4th row – P.
These 4 rows form patt.
Continue in patt until Back measures approx 24 cm, ending with 3rd row of patt.
Next row – Patt to end, cast on 39 [40,41] sts for sleeve. *183 [191,199] sts.*
Next row – (K1, P1) 3 times, K1, (yfwd, sl1, K2 tog, psso, yfwd, K1) 3 times, *K9 [10,11], (yfwd, sl1, K2 tog, psso, yfwd, K1) 3 times*; rep from * to * 3 times more, K8, rep from * to * 3 times more, K9 [10,11], cast on 39 [40,41] sts for sleeve. *222 [231,240] sts.*
1st row – (K1, P1) 3 times, P to last 6 sts, (P1, K1) 3 times.
2nd row – (K1, P1) 3 times, K to last 6 sts, (P1, K1) 3 times.
3rd row – As 1st.
4th row – (K1, P1) 3 times, K1, (yfwd, sl1, K2 tog, psso, yfwd, K1) 3 times, * K9 [10,11], (yfwd, sl1, K2 tog, psso, yfwd, K1) 3 times *; rep from * to * 5 times more, (P1, K1) 3 times.
Continue in patt until work measures 21 [22,23] cm from cast-on sleeve sts, ending with right side facing

for next row, and dec 1 st at centre of last row on 1st and 3rd sizes only. *221 [231,239] sts.*
Next row – Patt 91 [95,99], (K1, P1) 19 [20,20] times, K1, patt 91 [95,99]. Keeping patt correct and working centre 39 [41,41] sts in moss st continue thus until Back measures 23 [24,25] cm from cast-on sleeve sts, ending with wrong side facing for next row.
Cast off.

LOWER BAND

With No. 2¼ mm needles, cast on 53 sts and work as follows:
1st row – K1, *P1, K1; rep from * to end.
Rep last row until band fits around lower body, placing one side edge level with waist. Place a marker at each end of last row.
Work 2 rows.
Work buttonholes as follows:
Next 2 rows – Patt 3, *cast off 3, patt 8 (including st on needle after cast off)*; rep from * to * 3 times more, cast off 3, patt to end and back, casting on 3 sts over those cast off.
Work 2 rows.
Cast off.

TO MAKE UP

Do not press.
Join shoulder seams, then side and sleeve seams.
Place 18 sts at front edge of Right Front over top of 18 sts at front edge of Left Front and catch lower edges together.
Sew cast-on edges of Back and Fronts to one side edge of Lower Band, keeping open at left side and overlapping buttonhole piece so markers are level with cast-on edge, and easing fullness into band.
Cut elastic to fit waist and join in a ring. Sew inside top edge of Lower Band using herringbone stitch over elastic to form a casing.
Sew on buttons to correspond with buttonholes.

Note
A little time spent on careful make up of this design will be necessary to achieve a successful result.

JUMPER "ALMA" DESIGN

Linda

Woman's Sweater with Moss-stitch Front Detail (1924)

Elegant and sophisticated in fluffy wool; the subtle moss-stitch panelled neckline gives a certain dash to this charming blouson. Wear it with a mini-skirt for a flapper look or graced with pearls as in the photograph.

To fit bust		cm	81	86	91	97
	(approx)	in	32	34	36	38
Approximate length from top of shoulders		cm	66	66	67	68
		in	26	26	26½	27
Sleeve seam		cm	45	45	45	45
	(approx)	in	17½	17½	17½	17½
Patons Solo DK		50 g balls	7	7	8	8

Pair each Nos. 3¼ mm and 4 mm knitting needles.

Tension
On No. 4 mm needles, 22 sts and 29 rows to 10 cm (stocking stitch).

Abbreviations
K = knit; P = purl; st = stitch; tog = together; tbl = through back of loops; inc = increase; dec = decrease; M1 = make a stitch by picking up horizontal loop lying before next stitch and working into back of it; cm = centimetres; in = inches; mm = millimetres; rep = repeat; alt = alternate; patt = pattern; beg = beginning.

FRONT
With No. 3¼ mm needles, cast on 87 [93,99,105] sts and work in moss stitch as follows:
1st row – K1, *P1, K1; rep from * to end.
Rep last row 7 times more.

Change to No. 4 mm needles and, starting with a K row, work 24 rows stocking stitch.
Next row – K5 [8,6,9], (K2 tog tbl, K13 [13,15,15]) 3 times, (K2 tog, K13 [13,15,15]) twice, K2 tog, K5 [8,6,9]. *81 [87,93,99] sts.*
Work 5 rows.
Next row – K7 [5,8,6], (K2 tog tbl, K11 [13,13,15]) 3 times, (K2 tog, K11 [13,13,15]) twice, K2 tog, K7 [5,8,6]. *75 [81,87,93] sts.*
Work 5 rows.
Next row – K4 (7,5,8), (K2 tog tbl, K11 [11,13,13]) 3 times, (K2 tog, K11 [11,13,13]) twice, K2 tog, K4 [7,5,8]. *69 [75,81,87] sts.*
Work 1 row.

Change to No. 3¼ mm needles and work in rib for waist as follows:
1st row (right side) – K1, *P1, K1; rep from * to end.
2nd row – P1, *K1, P1; rep from * to end.
Rep last 2 rows 3 times more.

Change to No. 4 mm needles and work as follows:
Next row – K3 [6,9,1], (M1, K3 [3,3,4]) 21 times, M1, K3 [6,9,2]. *91 [97,103,109] sts.***
Starting with a P row, work 23 rows stocking stitch.
Work moss st patt as follows:
1st row – K45 [48,51,54], P1, K to end.
2nd row – P.
3rd row – As 1st.
4th row – P44 [48,50,53], K1, P1, K1, P to end.
Rep 3rd and 4th rows again.
7th row – K43 [46,49,52], (P1, K1) twice, P1, K to end.
8th row – As 4th.
Rep 7th and 8th rows again.
11th row – As 7th.
12th row – P42 [45,48,51], (K1, P1) 3 times, K1, P to end.
Rep 11th and 12th rows again.
15th row – K41 [44,47,50], (P1, K1) 4 times, P1, K to end.
16th row – As 12th.
Rep 15th and 16th rows again.
Continue taking 1 st more at each side into moss st patt until the 4 rows with 29 sts in moss st have been completed, and 58 patt rows have been worked.

Keeping patt correct, **shape armhole and divide for neck** as follows:
1st row – Cast off 3 sts, K25 [28,31,34] (including st

PATONS & BALDWINS

JUMPER.-"LINDA" DESIGN

on needle after cast off), K2 tog, (K1, P1) 7 times, K1, turn and leave remaining sts on a spare needle.

Continue on these 41 [44,47,50] sts for **left side** as follows:
2nd row – K1, (P1, K1) 7 times, P to end.
3rd row – K2 tog, K to last 14 sts, (P1, K1) 7 times.
4th row – K1, (P1, K1) 7 times, P to last 2 sts, P2 tog.
5th row – K2 tog, K to last 17 sts, K2 tog, K1, (P1, K1) 7 times.
6th row – K1, (P1, K1) 7 times, P to last 0 [2,2,2] sts, P2 tog 0 [1,1,1] time.
7th row – As 3rd.
8th row – K1 (P1, K1) 7 times, P to last 0 [0,0,2] sts, P2 tog 0 [0,0,1] time.
9th row – As 5th.
10th row – As 2nd.
11th row – As 3rd.
12th row – As 2nd.
13th row – As 5th.
14th row – As 2nd.
15th row – K2 tog 0 [1,1,1] time, K to last 14 sts, (P1, K1) 7 times.
16th row – As 2nd.
17th row – K2 tog 0 [0,1,1] time, K to last 17 sts, K2 tog, K1, [P1, K1] 7 times.
18th row – As 2nd.
19th row – K2 tog 0 [0,0,1] time, K to last 14 sts, (P1, K1) 7 times.
20th row – As 2nd.
21st row – K to last 17 sts, K2 tog, K1, (P1, K1) 7 times.
22nd row – As 2nd.
23rd row – K to last 14 sts, (P1, K1) 7 times.
Rep 20th to 23rd rows 8 [8,9,10] times more. Then 20th row again. 21 [22,23,23] sts.

2nd size only
Now rep 21st and 22nd rows again. 21 sts.

All sizes
Shape shoulder by casting off 7 sts at beg of next row, then 7 [7,8,8] sts at beg of following 2 alt rows.

With right side of work facing, rejoin yarn to remaining sts, cast off 1 st (thus leaving 1 st on right needle), (P1, K1) 7 times, K2 tog tbl, K to end.
2nd row – Cast off 3, P to last 15 sts, K1, (P1, K1) 7 times.
Complete to match left side, reversing shapings and

reading K2 tog tbl in place of the K2 tog by moss st patt only.

BACK
Work as for Front to **.
Starting with a P row, work 81 rows stocking stitch.

Shape armholes by casting off 3 sts at beg of next 2 rows, then dec 1 st at each end of next 3 [5,5,7] rows. Work 1 row.
Now dec 1 st at each end of next and following 3 [3,4,4] alt rows. 71 [73,77,79] sts.
Work 37 [37,37,39] rows straight, ending with a P row.
Next row – K7 [7,9,9], *P1, K1; rep from * to last 6 [6,8,8] sts, K6 [6,8,8].
Next row – P6 [6,8,8], *K1, P1; rep from * to last 5 [5,7,7] sts, P5 [5,7,7].
Rep last 2 rows twice more.

Keeping patt correct, **shape shoulders** by casting off 7 sts at beg of next 2 rows, then 7 [7,8,8] sts at beg of following 4 rows.
Cast off remaining 29 [31,31,33] sts.

SLEEVES
With No. 3¼ mm needles, cast on 41 [43,45,47] sts and work 8 rows in moss st as on Front.

Change to No. 4 mm needles and K 1 row, inc 3 sts evenly across row. 44 [46,48,50] sts.
Starting with a P row, work 11 [7,7,5] rows stocking stitch. Continue in stocking stitch, **shaping sides** by inc 1 st at each end of next and every following 13th [12th,12th,11th] row until there are 62 [66,68,72] sts.
Work straight until sleeve seam measures 45 cm, ending with a P row.

Shape top by casting off 3 sts at beg of next 2 rows, then dec 1 st at each end of next and following 4th row.
Work 3 rows.
Now dec 1 st at each end of next and every alt row until 22 sts remain.
Cast off.

TO MAKE UP
Omitting ribbing and moss st, press lightly on wrong side, following instructions given on yarn bands. Join shoulder, side and sleeve seams; insert sleeves. Press seams.

Scarves

(1924)

Three classic scarves from the twenties. Two are in simple rib to make as long or short as you please; the distinctive striped scarf, knitted on the diagonal, is not as difficult as it looks – we made it to match the hat on p. 63.

Abbreviations

K = knit; P = purl; st = stitch; tog = together; inc = increase; dec = decrease, beg = beginning; alt = alternate; rep = repeat; patt = pattern; cm = centimetres; in = inches; mm = millimetres; A = main shade; B = 1st contrast; C = 2nd contrast.

DESIGN A
Materials
3 50 g balls Patons Cotton Top or Solo DK.
Pair No. 4 mm needles.

Measurements
Length: 119 cm (47 in approx), excluding fringe.
Width: 25 cm (10 in approx).

Tension
25 sts and 30 rows to 10 cm (rib).

With No. 4 mm needles cast on 63 sts and work in rib as follows:
1st row – K2, *P1, K1; rep from * to last st, K1.
2nd row – K1, *P1, K1; rep from * to end.
Rep these 2 rows until work measures 119 cm.
Cast off evenly in rib.

Fringe
Take 6 strands of yarn, each 20 cm long, and fold in half; using crochet hook draw the loop through end of scarf. Pass ends through loop and knot firmly. Rep evenly along both ends of scarf.

DESIGN B
Materials
3 50 g balls Beehive DK.
Pair No. 4 mm needles.

Measurements
Length: 116 cm (45½ in approx), excluding fringe.
Width: 25 cm (10 in approx).

Tension
26 sts and 30 rows to 10 cm (rib).

With No. 4 mm needles cast on 65 sts and work in patt as follows:

1st row – *K2, P2; rep from * to last st, K1.
Rep this row until scarf measures 116 cm.
Cast off in patt.

Fringe
Work as given for Design A.

DESIGN C
Materials
3 50 g balls Moorland DK, shade A.
1 50 g ball Moorland DK, shade B.
1 50 g ball Moorland DK, shade C.
Pair No. 4 mm needles.

Measurements
Length: 116 cm (45½ in approx).

Tension
23 sts and 30 rows to 10 cm (patt).

With No. 4 mm needles and A, cast on 53 sts and work in patt as follows:
**1st row – In A, *K1, P1; rep from * to last st, P1.
2nd row – In A, P2 tog, *K1, P1; rep from * to last 3 sts, K1, inc in next st, P1.
3rd row – In A, *P1, K1; rep from * to last st, K1.
4th row – In A, K2 tog, *P1, K1; rep from * to last 3 sts, P1, inc in next st, K1.**
Rep from ** to ** 3 times more, then 1st row again.
Join in B and work as follows:
***1st row – (K1, P1) twice, K1, K2 tog, K to last 7 sts, inc in next st, K1 (K1, P1) twice, K1.
2nd row – (K1, P1) twice, K1, P to last 5 sts, (K1, P1) twice, K1.***
Rep from *** to *** working in stripes as follows:
2 more rows in B, 6 rows in C, 4 rows in B, 2 rows in A, 6 rows in B, 10 rows in C, 6 rows in B and 2 rows in A.
Break off A and B yarns.
Using C only, rep from *** to *** until work measures 102 cm from beg, ending with a 2nd row. Keeping continuity of patt, work in stripes of 2 rows in A, 6 rows in B, 10 rows in C, 6 rows in B, 2 rows in A, 4 rows in B, 6 rows in C, 4 rows in B and 1 row in A.
Break off B and C yarns.
Rep from ** to ** 4 times. Cast off.
Darn ends in neatly at sides of work.

Ina

Woman's Jumper (1925)

Chic and sweet, this head-turning asymmetrical jumper looks good with trousers or a straight skirt; it can be worn under a suit jacket in cool weather or on its own when the weather is warmer.

To fit bust		cm	81	86	91	97
(approx)	in	32	34	36	38
Length from top of shoulders		cm	54	55	57	58
(approx)	in	21½	21¾	22½	23
Sleeve seam		cm	7	7	7	7
(approx)	in	3	3	3	3
Patons Clansman 4 ply						
1st contrast (A)	50 g balls	1	1	1	1
2nd contrast (B)	50 g balls	1	1	2	2
Main colour (C)	50 g balls	3	3	4	4

Pair each Nos. 2¾ mm and 3¼ mm needles. A No. 2¾ mm circular pin.

Tension

On No. 3¼ mm needles, 28 sts and 36 rows to 10 cm (stocking stitch).

Abbreviations

K = knit; P = Purl; st = stitch; tog = together; inc = increase; dec = decrease; beg = beginning; alt = alternate; rep = repeat; patt = pattern; cm = centimetres; in = inches; mm = millimetres; A = 1st contrast; B = 2nd contrast; C = main shade.

FRONT

**With No. 2¾ mm needles and A cast on 113 [121,127,135] sts and work in rib, changing colours as follows:
1st row (right side) – K1, *P1, K1; rep from * to end.
2nd row – P1, *K1, P1; rep from * to end.
Rep 1st and 2nd rows once more. Break A.
Join B.
Work 2 more rows in rib. Break B.
Join C.
Work in rib until work measures 9 [9,10,10] cm, ending with a 2nd row.
Break C.
Join A.**

Change to No. 3¼ mm needles and K 1 row.
Divide for Fronts as follows.

Next row – P94 [100,105,111], turn and leave remaining sts on a spare needle.

Right side – Starting with a K row, work 2 rows in stocking stitch. Break A, and join B, work 2 rows. Break B, join C.
Continue in stocking stitch, shaping front slope by dec 1 st at beg of next row and on every following 3rd row at the same edge until 73 [79,84,90] sts remain. Work 1 row, then dec 1 st at same edge on next and every alt row until 62 [68,73,79] sts remain, ending with a K row.

Shape armhole by casting off 4 [4,5,5] sts at beg of next row.
Dec 1 st at each end of next and every alt row until 44 [46,48,50] sts remain.
Continue dec 1 st at front slope *only* on every alt row until 34 [34,33,33] sts remain. Work 3 rows. Now dec 1 st at front slope on next and every following 4th row until 25 [26,26,28] sts remain.
Work 2 rows, ending with a K row.

Shape shoulder by casting off 8 [9,9,9] sts at beg of next and following alt row. Work 1 row.
Cast off remaining 9 [8,8,10] sts.

With wrong side facing, using No. 3¼ mm needles and A, join yarn to sts from spare needle and cast on 75 [79,83,87] sts; P across these sts, P to end. 94 [100,105,111] sts.

PATONS & BALDWINS' HELPS TO KNITTERS No 352

LADIES' JUMPERS

FROM "VERONICA" SHOWERPROOF WOOL MADE BY

PATONS & BALDWINS, LTD.
ALLOA & HALIFAX

PUBLISHED WITH ALL RIGHTS RESERVED

PRICE 2d

Starting with a K row work 2 rows in stocking stitch.
Break A, join B and work 2 rows.
Continue in stocking stitch, **shaping front slope** by
dec 1 st at *end* of next row and on every following
3rd row at the same edge until 73 [79,84,90] sts
remain. Work 1 row, then dec 1 st at same edge on
next and every alt row until 63 [69,74,80] sts
remain.
Work 1 row.

Shape armhole – Cast off 4 [4,5,5] sts, K to last 2 sts,
K 2 tog.
Work 1 row.
Dec 1 st at each end of next and every alt row until
44 [46,48,50] sts remain.
Work 1 row.

1st, 2nd, and 3rd sizes only
Continue dec 1 st at front slope *only* on next and
every alt row until 39 [43,46] sts remain.

All sizes
Work 1 row.
Break B, join A.
Work 4 rows, dec 1 st at front slope as before.
Break A, join B.
Work 2 rows, dec 1 st at front slope as before.
Break B, join C.
Continuing dec 1 st at front slope on next and every
alt row until 34 [34,33,33] sts remain.
Work 3 rows.
Now dec 1 st at front slope on next and every
following 4th row until 25 [26,26,28] sts remain.
Work 1 row.
Shape shoulder as for right side.

BACK
Work as for Front from ** to **.

Change to No. 3¼ mm needles and, starting with a K
row work 4 rows in A.
Break A, join B.
Work 2 rows.
Break B, join C and work 84 rows.

Shape armhole by casting off 4 [4,5,5] sts at beg of
next 2 rows. Dec 1 st at each end of next and every
alt row until 91 [95,97,101] sts remain.
Work straight until Back matches Front to start of
shoulder shaping, ending with a P row.

Shape shoulders by casting off 8 [9,9,9] sts at beg of
next 4 rows, then 9 [8,8,9] sts at beg of next 2 rows.
Leave remaining 41 [43,45,47] sts on a spare needle.

SLEEVES
With No. 2¾ mm needles and A cast on 65
[67,71,75] sts and work 4 rows in rib as for Front.
Break A, join B and work 1 row in rib.
Next row – Rib 5 [1,3,5], * inc in next st, rib 4; rep
from * to last 5 [1,3,5] sts, inc in next st, rib to end.
77 [81,85,89] sts.
Break B, join C.

Change to No. 3¼ mm needles and, starting with a K
row, work in stocking stitch, shaping sides by inc 1 st
at each end of 3rd and every following 4th row until
there are 87 [91,95,99] sts.
Work straight until sleeve seam measures 7 cm,
ending with a P row.

Shape top by casting off 4 [4,5,5] sts at beg of next 2
rows. Dec 1 st at each end of next and every
following 4th row until 69 [73,75,79] sts remain.
Work 1 row.
Dec 1 st at each end of next and every alt row until
41 [41,37,37] sts remain.
Work 1 row.
Dec 1 st at each end of every row until 25 sts
remain.
Cast off.

FRONT BORDER
With right side facing, No. 2¾ mm circular pin and B,
knit up 112 [116,120,124] sts evenly along edge of
right front slope to shoulder, K across 41 [43,45,47]
sts from spare needle at back neck, then knit up 112
[116,120,124] sts evenly down left front slope. *265
[275,285,295] sts.*
Work backwards and forwards as follows:
1st row (wrong side) – P1, * K1, P1; rep from * to
end.
Break B, join A.
2nd row – K1, *P1, K1; rep from * to end.
3rd row – As 1st.
4th row – As 2nd.
5th row – As 1st.
Cast off evenly in rib.

TO MAKE UP
Press, following instructions on the yarn label. Join
the cast-on sts of left front to wrong side of work
above rib.
Join shoulder, side and sleeve seams.
Insert sleeves.
Press seams.

Ina

Alma

Linda

Sam

Turban, Scarf and Gauntlet Gloves

Betty

Woman's Sweater (1927)

A sensation on the ice-rink or for après-ski – *indeed anywhere where you want to be noticed! Knit this jumper in bold primary colours or change the mood with more sophisticated contrasts. It is easy and quick to knit in stocking stitch with double knitting yarn.*

			81	86	91	97
To fit bust		cm	81	86	91	97
	(approx)	in	32	34	36	38
Length from top of shoulders		cm	59	60	61	62
	(approx)	in	23	23½	24	24½
Sleeve seam, with cuff turned back		cm	43	43	44	44
	(approx)	in	17	17	17½	17½
Patons Clansman DK						
Main colour (A)		50 g balls	8	8	9	9
1st contrast (B)		50 g balls	2	2	2	2
2nd contrast (C)		50 g balls	1	1	2	2

Pair each Nos. 3¼ mm and 4 mm needles.
5 No. 3¼ mm needles with points at both ends.

Tension
On No. 4 mm needles, 22 sts and 30 rows to 10 cm (stocking stitch).

Abbreviations
K = knit; P = purl; st = stitch; tog = together; tbl = through back of loop; beg = beginning; alt = alternate; rep = repeat; patt = pattern; inc = increase; dec = decrease; cm = centimetres; in = inches; mm = millimetres; M1 = make a stitch by picking up horizontal loop lying before next stitch and working into back of it; A = main shade; B = 1st contrast; C = 2nd contrast.

Note
When working colour patt, use separate balls of yarn, twisting yarn on wrong side when changing colour to avoid a hole.

FRONT
** With No. 3¼ mm needles and B, cast on 91 [97,103,109] sts, and work in rib as follows:
1st row (right side) – K1, *P1, K1; rep from * to end.
2nd row – P1, * K1, P1; rep from * to end.
Rep 1st and 2nd rows twice more.

Break B, join C, and work 6 rows in rib. Break C and join B. Work 6 rows in rib, inc 1 st in centre of last row. *91 [98,104,110] sts.*
Break B, join A.**

Change to No. 4 mm needles. Starting with a K row, work 4 rows in stocking stitch.
Joining in and breaking off colours as required, work as follows:
1st row – K73 [76,79,82] in A, 18 in B, 1 [4,7,10] in A.
2nd row – P1 [4,7,10] in A, 18 in B, 73 [76,79,82] in A.
Rep 1st and 2nd rows 5 times.
13th row – K64 [67,70,73] in A, 9 in C, 18 in B, 1 [4,7,10] in A.
14th row – P1 [4,7,10] in A, 18 in B, 9 in C, 64 [67,70,73] in A.
Rep 13th and 14th rows 5 times. Break B.
25th row – K64 [67,70,73] in A, 18 in C, 10 [13,16,19] in A.
26th row – P10 [13,16,19] in A, 18 in C, 64 [67,70,73] in A.
Rep 25th and 26th rows 5 times. Break C.
37th row – K in A.
38th row – P in A.
Rep 37th and 38th rows once.
41st row – K46 [49,52,55] in A, 18 in B, 28 [31,34,37] in A.

42nd row – P28 [31,34,37] in A, 18 in B, 46 [49,52,55] in A.
Rep 41st and 42nd rows 5 times.
53rd row – K37 [40,43,46] in A, 9 in C, 18 in B, 28 [31,34,37] in A.
54th row – P28 [31,34,37] in A, 18 in B, 9 in C, 37 [40,43,46] in A.
Rep 53rd and 54th rows 5 times. Break B.
65th row – K37 [40,43,46] in A, 18 in C, 37 [40,43,46] in A.
66th row – P37 [40,43,46] in A, 18 in C, 37 [40,43,46] in A.
Rep 65th and 66th rows 5 times. Break C.
77th row – K in A.
78th row – P in A.
Rep 77th and 78th rows once.
81st row – K19 [22,25,28] in A, 18 in B, 55 [58,61,64] in A.
82nd row – P55 [58,61,64] in A, 18 in B, 19 [22,25,28] in A.
Rep 81st and 82nd rows 5 times.
93rd row – K10 [13,16,19] in A, 9 in C, 18 in B, 55 [58,61,64] in A.
94th row – P55 [58,61,64] in A, 18 in B, 9 in C, 10 [13,16,19] in A.
Rep 93rd and 94th rows once.

Keeping continuity of patt, **shape armholes** by casting off 3 [3,4,4] sts at beg of next 2 rows, then dec 1 st at each end of next and every alt row until 72 [76,80,84] sts remain.
Work 5 [3,3,1] row. Break C.
Continue in stocking stitch and A until armhole measures 9 [10,11,12] cm, ending with a P row.

Divide for neck – K20 [22,24,26], turn and leave remaining sts on a spare needle.

Left side – Work 1 row on these sts. Dec 1 st at neck edge on next and every following 6th row until 16 [17,18,19] sts remain.
Work straight until armhole measures 20 [21,22,23] cm, ending with a P row.

Shape shoulder by casting off 5 [6,6,6] sts at beg of next and following alt row.
Work 1 row.
Cast off remaining 6 [5,6,7] sts.

With right side facing, slip centre 32 [34,36,38] sts on to a length of yarn. Rejoin yarn to remaining sts and K to end.
Complete to match left side, reversing shapings.

BACK
Work as for Front from ** to **.

Change to No. 4 mm needles. Using A throughout and starting with a K row, work in stocking stitch until Back measures same as Front to start of armhole shaping.

Shape armholes by casting off 3 [3,4,4] sts at beg of next 2 rows. Dec 1 st at each end of next and every alt row until 72 [76,80,84] sts remain. Work straight until 6 rows less than Front have been worked to start of shoulder shaping, ending with a P row.

Divide for neck – K16 [17,18,19], turn and leave remaining sts on a spare needle. Work 5 rows on these sts.

Shape shoulder by casting off 5 [6,6,6] sts at beg of next and following alt row. Cast off remaining 6 [5,6,7] sts.
With right side facing, slip centre 40 [42,44,46] sts on to a length of yarn. Rejoin yarn to remaining sts. K to end.
Complete to match first side, reversing shapings.

SLEEVES
With No. 3¼ mm needles and B cast on 43 [45,47,49] sts and work 6 rows in rib as for Front. Break B, join C and work 6 rows rib. Break C, join B and work 6 rows in rib. Break B, join A and work 16 rows in rib.
Next row – Rib 4 [3,3,4], *M1, rib 7 [8,6,6]; rep from * to last 4 [2,2,3] sts, M1, rib to end. 49 [51,55,57] sts.

Change to No. 4 mm needles. Starting with a K row, work in stocking stitch, shaping sides by inc 1 st at each end of 3rd [3rd,5th,5th] and every following 10th row until there are 69 [71,75,77] sts.
Work straight until sleeve seam measures 48 [48,49,49] cm, ending with a P row.

Shape top by casting off 3 [3,4,4] sts at beg of next 2 rows. Dec 1 st at each end of next and every alt row until 41 [37,37,33] sts remain.
Work 1 row.
Now dec 1 st at each end of every row until 21 sts remain.
Cast off.

TO MAKE UP – NECK BORDER
Join shoulder seams.
With right side facing, using the No. 3¼ mm needles

PATONS & BALDWINS

with points at both ends and B, start at right corner of back neck and with first needle K40 [42,44,46] sts from back, inc 1 st at centre. With second needle knit up 29 sts down left side of neck; with third needle K32 [34,36,38] sts from front, inc 1 st at centre; with fourth needle knit up 29 sts up right side of neck. *132 [136,140,144] sts.*

Work in rib as follows.

1st round – K2 tog, (P1, K1) 18 [19,20,21] times, P1, K2 tog tbl, K2 tog, (P1, K1) 12 times, P1, K2 tog tbl, K2 tog, (P1, K1) 14 [15,16,17] times, P1, K2 tog tbl, K2 tog, (P1, K1) 12 times, P1, K2 tog tbl.

Keeping continuity of rib, dec 1 st at each end of each needle in every round, working stripes as follows – 1 more round in B, 4 rounds in C and 2 rounds in B. Cast off evenly in rib.

Join side and sleeve seams.

Insert sleeves. Turn sleeve cuff in half to right side.

Gauntlet Gloves

(1930s)

Look chic and stay warm in winter. These superb gloves can be matched with any of the hats and scarves in this book.

Materials
2 50 g balls Patons Clansman 4ply.
Set of 4 No. 3¼ mm needles with points at both ends.

Measurements
To fit average woman's hand.

Tension
28 sts and 36 rows to 10 cm (stocking st).

Abbreviations
K = knit; P = purl; st = stitch; tog = together; inc = increase; dec = decrease; beg = beginning; mm = millimetres.

RIGHT GLOVE
Cast on 160 sts, 53 on the first two needles and 54 on the third.
Mark first st with coloured thread to denote beg of round and work in rounds as follows:
1st round – * P2, K6; rep from * to end.
Rep this round 8 times more.
Next round – * P2, K2, K2 tog, K2; rep from * to end. *140 sts.*
Next round – * P2, K5; rep from * to end.
Rep last round 8 times more.
Next round – * P2, K2, K2 tog, K1; rep from * to end. *120 sts.*
Next round – * P2, K4; rep from * to end.
Rep last round 8 times more.
Next round – * P2, K1, K2 tog, K1; rep from * to end. *100 sts.*
Next round – * P2, K3; rep from * to end.
Rep last round 8 times more.
Next round – * P2 tog, K3 tog; rep from * to end. *40 sts.*
Next round – * P1, K1; rep from * to end.
Rep last round 9 times more.
Next round – * K5, inc in next st; rep from * to end. *48 sts.*
Work in stocking stitch (every round knit) from here on. Work 2 rounds.**

Shape thumb gusset
Next round – K1, inc once in each of the next 2 sts, K to end.
Work 3 rounds.
Next round – K1, inc in next st, K2, inc in next st, K to end.
Work 3 rounds.
Next round – K1, inc in next st, K4, inc in next st, K to end.
Continue in this way, inc in thumb gusset in every following 4th round until there are 60 sts.
Work 8 rounds on these sts.
Next round – K1, slip next 14 sts on to a length of yarn and leave for thumb, cast on 5 sts, K to end.
Work 14 rounds.

Note. When working fingers and thumb, sts should be divided on to 3 needles.

First finger
K first 8 sts of round, slip all but last 6 sts on to a length of yarn and leave; cast on 2 sts, K last 6 sts. *16 sts.*
Work 30 rounds.
Shape top – K2 tog 8 times.
Work 1 more round. Break yarn, thread through remaining sts and fasten off.

Second finger
Rejoin yarn and K next 6 sts of round, cast on 2 sts, K last 7 sts of round, knit up 2 sts from base of first finger. *17 sts.*
Work 36 rounds.
Shape top – K1, (K2 tog) 8 times.
Complete as for first finger.

***Third finger
Rejoin yarn and K next 6 sts of round, cast on 2 sts, K last 6 sts of round, knit up 2 sts from base of second finger. *16 sts.*
Complete as for first finger.

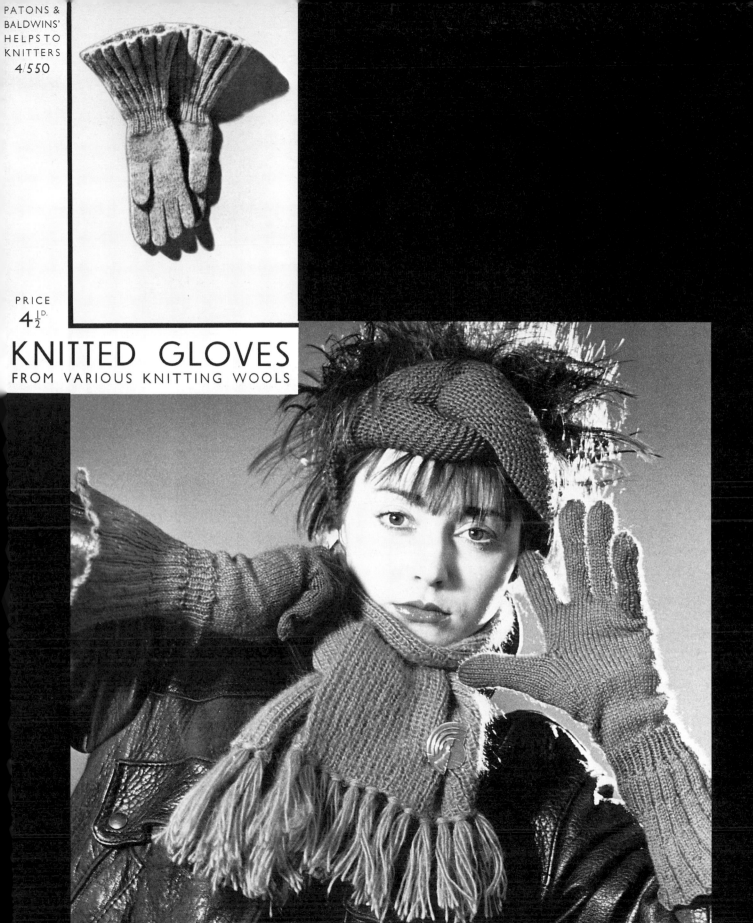

PATONS &
BALDWINS'
HELPS TO
KNITTERS
4/550

PRICE
4½ D.

KNITTED GLOVES
FROM VARIOUS KNITTING WOOLS

Fourth finger
Rejoin yarn and K remaining 12 sts of round, knit up 2 sts from base of third finger. *14 sts.*
Work 26 rounds.
Complete as for first finger. ***

Thumb
K14 sts from length of yarn, knit up 5 sts from cast-on sts. *19 sts.*
Work 26 rounds.
Shape top and complete as for second finger.

LEFT GLOVE
Work as Right Glove to **.

Shape thumb gusset
Next round – K to last 3 sts, inc once in each of next 2 sts, K1.
Work 3 rounds.
Next round – K to last 5 sts, inc in next st, K2, inc in next st, K1.
Work 3 rounds.
Next round – K to last 7 sts, inc in next st, K4, inc in next st, K1.
Continue in this way, inc in thumb gusset in every following 4th round until there are 60 sts.
Work 8 rounds on these sts.
Next round – K to last 15 sts, cast on 5 sts, slip next

14 sts on to a length of yarn and leave for thumb, K1.
Work 14 rounds.

First finger
K first 6 sts of round, cast on 2 sts, slip all but last 8 sts on to a length of yarn and leave, K last 8 sts of round. *16 sts.*
Work 30 rounds.
Shape top as given for first finger of Right Glove.

Second finger
Rejoin yarn and K next 7 sts of round, cast on 2 sts, K last 6 sts of round, knit up 2 sts from base of first finger. *17 sts.*
Work 36 rounds.
Shape top – K1, (K2 tog) 8 times.
Complete as for first finger.

Work from *** to *** as for Right Glove.

Thumb
Knit up 5 sts from cast-on sts, K 14 sts from length of yarn. *19 sts.*
Work 26 rounds.
Shape top and complete as second finger.

TO FINISH
Press, following instructions on yarn label.

Cottage Tea Cosy

(1931)

Materials

2 50 g balls Patons Clansman DK in shade A.
2 50 g balls in shade B.
1 50 g ball in shade C.
Oddments of coloured yarns for embroidery.
Pair each Nos. 3¼ mm and 4 mm needles.
A No. 4 mm crochet hook.
8 pipe cleaners.

Measurements

Approx 22 × 10 cm (approx 8½ × 4 in).

Tension

On No. 4 mm needles, 22 sts and 32 rows to 10 cm
with yarn used double (patt).
On No. 3¼ mm needles, 23 sts and 32 rows to 10 cm
with yarn used double (stocking stitch).

Abbreviations

K = knit; P = purl; st = stitch; yft = yarn front –
bring yarn to front of needle; yb = yarn back – take
yarn to back of needle; tog = together; inc =
increase; dec = decrease; beg = beginning; alt =
alternate; rep = repeat; patt = pattern; cm =
centimetres; in = inches; mm = millimetres; M1 =
make a stitch by picking up horizontal loop lying
before next stitch and working into back of it; ch =
chain, dc = double crochet; sl1P = slip 1 stitch
purlwise.

WALLS: FRONT AND BACK (make 2)

With No. 4 mm needles and A yarn used double, cast
on 49 sts.
1st row (right side) – *K1, yft, sl1P, yb; rep from * to
last st, K1.
2nd row – P.
3rd row – K1, *K1, yft, sl1P, yb; rep from * to last 2
sts, K2.
4th row – P.
These 4 rows form patt.
Continue in patt until work measures 15 cm, ending
with a P row. Cast off.

Knit and embroider this nostalgic tea cosy – your
very own dream cottage!

SIDE WALLS (make 2)

With No. 4 mm needles and A yarn used double, cast
on 23 sts. Work in patt as for Front and Back Walls
until work measures 15 cm, ending with a P row.
Cast off.

ROOF: FRONT AND BACK (make 2)

With No. 3¼ mm needles and B yarn used double,
cast on 11 sts.
1st row – (right side) – Inc in first st, K to last 2 sts,
inc in next st, K1.
2nd row – Inc in first st, P to last 2 sts, inc in next
st, P1.
3rd row As 1st.
4th row – P.
Rep 1st to 4th rows 4 times more, then 1st to 3rd
rows once. *47 sts.*
Next row – Inc in first st, P18, cast off 9, P to last 2
sts, inc in next st, P1.
Continue on first 20 sts as follows:
1st row – Inc in first st, K to end.
2nd row – Cast off 2, P to last 2 sts, inc in next st,
P1.
3rd row – K.
4th row – As 2nd.
5th row – As 1st.
6th row – As 2nd.
7th row – K.
8th row – Cast off 1, P to last 2 sts, inc in next st,
P1.
9th row – As 1st.
10th row – Cast off 4, P to last 2 sts, inc in next st,
P1.
11th row – K.
12th row – As 10th.
Cast off.
With right side facing, rejoin yarn to remaining sts. K
to last 2 sts, inc in next st, K1.
Finish to match first side, reversing shapings.

ROOF: SIDES (make 2)

With No. 3¼ mm needles and B yarn used double,
cast on 3 sts, and K 1 row.

Continue in stocking stitch, inc 1 st at each end of every row until there are 43 sts. Work 6 rows. Cast off.

WATERBUTT
With No. 3¼ mm needles and B yarn, cast on 11 sts.
Starting with a K row, work 4 rows in stocking stitch. Inc 1 st at each end of next and following 4th row.
Work 7 rows in stocking stitch.
Dec 1 st at each end of next and following 4th row.
Work 1 row.
Cast off.

FRONT AND BACK DOORS (make 2)
With No. 3¼ mm needles and C yarn, cast on 14 sts.
1st row – (K4, P1) twice, K4.
2nd row – K1, P3, K1, P4, K1, P3, K1.
Rep these 2 rows 10 times.
Cast off.

SHUTTERS (make 2)
With No. 3¼ mm needles and C yarn, cast on 5 sts.
Starting with a K row, work 14 rows in stocking stitch.
Cast off.

CHIMNEY
With No. 3¼ mm needles and A yarn cast on 24 sts.
Starting with a K row, work 4 rows in stocking stitch.
Next row – (K6, M1) 3 times, K6. *27 sts.*
Work 3 rows.

Next row – (K5, K2 tog) 3 times, K6.
Work 3 rows.
Cast off.

TO MAKE UP
With wrong side of work facing, block each piece by pinning out round edges. Press, following the instructions given on yarn bands.
Using back stitch, join walls and roof sections, leaving space in centre for chimney. Join chimney seam and sew in position. Press seams.

Roof edging
With a No. 4 mm crochet hook and B yarn, make a length of ch loosely, long enough to fit all round edge of roof.
Work in ch as follows:
Insert hook into 2nd ch from hook, * slip first finger of left hand under hook, wrap yarn round hook and finger twice, yarn over hook, draw a loop through 2 loops and ch, yarn over hook and draw a loop through remaining 2 loops, 1 dc in next ch; rep from * to end.
Stitch edging all round roof, join roof to walls, overlapping slightly all round.

To finish
Stitch doors, shutters and waterbutt in position and work embroidery as illustrated.
Bind 2 pipe cleaners together with A yarn and sew in position down one corner of inside walls for support.
Bind remaining pipe cleaners in pairs and sew in other corners in same way.

Man's Sweater (1932)

An effective diamond pattern adds interest to this cropped-waist pullover with its thirties neckline. If it doesn't grow fast enough, you could change course midstream and make the sleeveless version instead. (Instructions on p. 39.)

To fit chest					
		cm	91–7	102–7	112–17
(approx)		in	36–8	40–42	44–46
Length from top of shoulder		cm	63	66	68
(approx)		in	25	26	27
Sleeve seam		cm	46	47	48
(approx)		in	18	18½	19
Patons Clansman DK					
For Sweater		50 g balls	12	13	14
For Sleeveless Pullover		50 g balls	9	10	10

Pair each Nos. 3¼ mm and 4 mm needles.

Tension
On No. 4 mm needles, 22 sts and 30 rows to 10 cm (patt).

Abbreviations
K = knit; P = purl; st = stitch; yrn = yarn round needle; tog = together; yon = yarn over needle; inc = increase; dec = decrease; beg = beginning; alt = alternate; rep = repeat; patt = pattern; cm = centimetres; in = inches; mm = millimetres; MI = make a stitch by picking up horizontal loop lying before next st and working into back of it.

BACK
**With No. 3¼ mm needles, cast on 101 [113,121] sts and work in rib as follows:
1st row – right side – K1, *P1, K1; rep from * to end.
2nd row – P1, *K1, P1; rep from * to end.
Rep these 2 rows until work measures 7 [8,8] cm, ending with a 1st row.
Next row – Rib 6 [7,8], * MI, rib 10 [11,12]; rep from * to last 5 [7,7] sts, MI, rib to end. *111 [123,133] sts.*

Change to No. 4 mm needles and work in patt as follows:
1st row – right side – P10 [7,12], * yrn, P2 tog, P16; rep from * to last 11 [8,13] sts, yrn, P2 tog, P9 [6,11].
2nd row – K10 [7,12], * P1, K17; rep from * to last 11 [8,13] sts, P1, K10 [7,12].
3rd row – P8 [5,10], * P2 tog, yrn, K1, yrn, P2 tog, P13; rep from * to last 13 [10,15] sts, P2 tog, yrn, K1, yrn, P2 tog, P8 [5,10].
4th row – K9 [6,11], * P3, K15; rep from * to last 12 [9,14] sts, P3, K9 [6,11].
5th row – P7 [4,9], * P2 tog, yrn, K3, yrn, P2 tog, P11; rep from * to last 14 [11,16] sts, P2 tog, yrn, K3, yrn, P2 tog, K7 [4,9].
6th row – K8 [5,10], * P5, K13; rep from * to last 13[10,15] sts, P5, K8 [5,10].
7th row – P6 [3,8], * P2 tog, yrn, K5, yrn, P2 tog, P9; rep from * to last 15[12,17] sts, P2 tog, yrn, K5, yrn, P2 tog, P6 [3,8].
8th row – K7 [4,9], * P7, K11; rep from * to last 14 [11,16] sts, P7, K7 [4,9].
9th row – P5 [2,7], *P2 tog, yrn, K7, yrn, P2 tog, P7; rep from * to last 16 [13,18] sts, P2 tog, yrn, K7, yrn, P2 tog, P5 [2,7].
10th row – K6 [3,8], * P9, K9; rep from * to last 15 [12,17] sts, P9, K6 [3,8].
11th row – P4 [1,6], * P2 tog, yrn, K9, yrn, P2 tog, P5; rep from * to last 17 [14,19] sts, P2 tog, yrn, K9, yrn, P2 tog, K4 [1,6].
12th row – K5 [2,7], * P11, K7; rep from * to last 16 [13,18] sts, P11, K5 [2,7].
13th row – P3 [0,5], * P2 tog, yrn, K11, yrn, P2 tog, P3; rep from * to last 18 [15,20] sts, P2 tog, yrn, K11, yrn, P2 tog, P3 [0,5].
14th row – K4 [1,6], * P13, K5; rep from * to last 17 [14,19] sts, P13, K4 [1,6].

15th row – P5 [2,7], * K11, P7; rep from * to last 16 [13,18] sts, K11, P5 [2,7].

16th row – K5 [2,7], * P11, K7; rep from * to last 16 [13,18] sts, P11, K5 [2,7].

17th row – P6 [3,8], * K9, P9; rep from * to last 15 [12,17] sts, K9, P6 [3,8].

18th row – K6 [3,8], * P9, K9; rep from * to last 15 [12,17] sts, P9, K6 [3,8].

19th row – P7 [4,9], * K7, P11; rep from * to last 14 [11,16] sts, K7, P7 [4,9].

20th row – K7 [4,9], * P7, K11; rep from * to last 14 [11,16] sts, P7, K7 [4,9].

21st row – P8 [5,10], * K5, P13; rep from * to last 13 [10,15] sts, K5, P8 [5,10].

22nd row – K8 [5,10], * P5, K13; rep from * to last 13 [10,15] sts, P5, K8 [5,10].

23rd row – P9 [6,11], * K3, P15; rep from * to last 12 [9,14] sts, K3, P9 [6,11].

24th row – K9 [6,11], * P3, K13; rep from * to last 12 [9,14] sts, P3, K9 [6,11].

25th row – P10 [7,12], * K1, P11; rep from * to last 11 [8,13] sts, K1, P10 [7,12].

26th row – K10 [7,12], * P1, K11; rep from * to last 11 [8,13] sts, P1, K10 [7,12].

27th row – P19 [16,21], * yrn, P2 tog, P16; rep from * to last 20 [17,22] sts, yrn, P2 tog, P18 [15,20].

28th row – K19 [16,21], * P1, K17; rep from * to last 20 [17,22] sts, P1, K19 [16,21].

29th row – P17 [14,19], * P2 tog, yrn, K1, yrn, P2 tog, P13; rep from * to last 22 [19,24] sts, P2 tog, yrn, K1, yrn, P2 tog, P17 [14,19].

30th row – K18 [15,10], *P3, K15; rep from * to last 21 [18,13] sts, P3, K18 [15,10].

31st row – P16 [13,18], * P2 tog, yrn, K3, yrn, P2 tog, P11; rep from * to last 23 [20,25] sts, P2 tog, yrn, K3, yrn, P2 tog, P16 [13,18].

32nd row – K17 [14,19], * P5, K13; rep from * to last 22 [19,24] sts, P5, K17 [14,19].

33rd row – P15 [12,17], * P2 tog, yrn, K5, yrn, P2 tog, P9; rep from * to last 24 [21,26] sts, P2 tog, yrn, K5, yrn, P2 tog, P15 [12,17].

34th row – K16 [13,18], * P7, K11; rep from * to last 23 [20,25] sts, P7, K16 [13,18].

35th row – P14 [11,16], * P2 tog, yrn, K7, yrn, P2 tog, P7; rep from * to last 25 [22,27] sts, P2 tog, yrn, K7, yrn, P2 tog, P14 [11,16].

36th row – K15 [12,17], * P9, K9; rep from * to last 24 [21,26] sts, P9, K15 [12,17].

37th row – P13 [10,15], * P2 tog, yrn, K9, yrn, P2 tog, P5; rep from * to last 26 [23,28] sts, P2 tog, yrn, K9, yrn, P2 tog, P13 [10,15].

38th row – K14 [11,16], * P11, K7; rep from * to last 25 [22,27] sts, P11, K14 [11,16].

39th row – P12 [9,14], * P2 tog, yrn, K11, yrn, P2 tog, P3; rep from * to last 27 [24,29] sts, P2 tog, yrn, K11, yrn, P2 tog, P12 [9,14].

40th row – K13 [10,15], * P13, K5; rep from * to last 26 [23,28] sts, P13, K13 [10,15].

41st row – P14 [11,16], * K11, P7; rep from * to last 25 [22,27] sts, K11, P14 [11,16].

42nd row – K14 [11,16], * P11, K7; rep from * to last 25 [22,27] sts, P11, K14 [11,16].

43rd row – P15 [12,17], *K9, P9; rep from * to last 24 [21,26] sts, K9, P15 [12,17].

44th row – K15 [12,17], * P9, K9; rep from * to last 24 [21,26] sts, P9, K15 [12,17].

45th row – P16 [13,18], * K7, P11; rep from * to last 23 [20,25] sts, K7, P16 [13,18].

46th row – K16 [13,18], * P7, K11; rep from * to last 23 [20,25] sts, P7, K16 [13,18].

47th row – P17 [14,19], * K5, P13; rep from * to last 22 [19,24] sts, K5, P17 [14,19].

48th row – K17 [14,19], * P5, K13; rep from * to last 22 [19,24] sts, P5, K17 [14,19].

49th row – P18 [15,20], * K3, P15; rep from * to last 21 [18,23] sts, K3, P18 [15,20].

50th row – K18 [15,20], * P3, K15; rep from * to last 21 [18,23] sts, P3, K18 [15,20].

51st row – P19 [16,21], * K1, P17; rep from * to last 20 [17,22] sts, K1, P19 [16,21].

52nd row – K19 [16,21], * P1, K17; rep from * to last 20 [17,22] sts, P1, K19 [16,21].

These 52 rows form patt.

Continue in patt until Back measures 39 [40,40] cm, ending with right side facing for next row. **

Shape armholes by casting off 5 [6,6] sts at beg of next 2 rows. Dec 1 st at each end of next and every alt row until 89 [95,101] sts remain.

Work straight in patt until Back measures 63 [66,68] cm, ending with right side facing for next row.

Shape shoulders by casting off 8[9,9] sts at beg of next 4 rows, then 8[8,9] sts at beg of following 2 rows.

Cast off remaining 41 [43,47] sts.

FRONT

Work as for Back from ** to **.

Keeping continuity of patt, **shape armholes** and beg front neck rib as follows:

1st row – Cast off 5 [6,6], patt 43 [48,53] (including st on needle after cast off), (K1, P1) 7 times, K1, patt to end.

2nd row – Cast off 5 [6,6], patt 43 [48,53] (including st on needle after cast off), (P1, K1) 7 times, P1, patt to end.

Keeping continuity of patt and 15 rib sts at centre, dec 1 st at each end of next and every alt row until 89 [99,109] sts remain, ending with wrong side facing for next row.

Divide for neck – Patt 37 [42,47], rib 7, cast off 1 st, rib 7 (including st on needle after cast off), patt 37 [42,47].

Work on last 44 [49,54] sts for first side, leave remaining sts on spare needle.

2nd and 3rd sizes only

1st row – Work 2 tog, patt to last 9 sts, P2 tog, rib 7.

2nd row – Rib 7, patt to end.

3rd row – Work 2 tog, patt to last 7 sts, rib 7.

4th row – As 2nd row.

3rd size only

Rep last 4 rows once more.

All sizes

1st row – Patt to last 9 sts, P2 tog, rib 7.

2nd row – Rib 7, patt to end.

3rd row – Patt to last 7 sts, rib 7.

4th row – As 2nd row.

Rep last 4 rows until 31 [33,34] sts remain.

Work straight until Front matches Back to start of shoulder shaping, ending with right side facing for next row.

Shape shoulder

1st row – Cast off 8 [9,9] sts, patt to last 7 sts, rib 7.

2nd row – Rib 7, patt to end.

Rep last 2 rows once more.

Next row – Cast off 8 [8,9], rib to end.

Continue in rib on remaining 7 sts until strip measures sufficient to fit across to centre back of neck. Cast off in rib.

With right side facing, rejoin yarn to remaining sts.

2nd and 3rd sizes only

1st row – Rib 7, P2 tog, patt to last 2 sts, work 2 tog.

2nd row – Patt to last 7 sts, rib 7.

3rd row – Rib 7, patt to last 2 sts, work 2 tog.

4th row – As 2nd row.

3rd size only

Rep last 4 rows once more.

All sizes

1st row – Rib 7, P2 tog, patt to end.

2nd row – Patt to last 7 sts, rib 7.

3rd row – Rib 7, patt to end.

4th row – As 2nd row.

Rep last 4 rows and complete to match first side, reversing shaping.

SLEEVES

With No. 3¼ mm needles, cast on 51 [53,55] sts and work 6 cm in rib as for Back, ending with a 1st row.

Next row – Rib 6 [2,5], * M1, rib 8 [7,9]; rep from * to last 5 [2,5] sts, M1, rib to end. *57 [61,61] sts.*

Change to No. 4 mm needles and work in patt as given for 1st [3rd,3rd] size of Back, shaping sides by inc 1 st at each end of 9th [7th,9th] and every following 6th [7th,6th] row, until there are 87 [91,95] sts, taking inc sts into patt.

Work straight until sleeve seam measures 46 [47,48] cm, ending with right side facing for next row.

Keeping continuity of patt, shape top by casting off 5 [6,6] sts at beg of next 2 rows.

Dec 1 st at each end of next row. Work 3 rows.

Rep last 4 rows 0 [1,2] times more.

Now dec 1 st at each end of next and every alt row until 23 sts remain. Work 1 row.

Cast off.

TO MAKE UP

Press, following instructions on yarn label.

Join shoulder, side and sleeve seams.

Insert sleeves.

Sew rib across back neck.

Join cast-off edges.

Press seams.

SLEEVELESS VERSION

Work back and front as above.

TO MAKE UP

Press as for Sweater.

Join shoulder seams, sew rib across back neck.

Join cast-off edges.

Armhole borders

With right side facing and No. 3¼ mm needles, knit up 107 [115,123] sts evenly round armhole. Starting with a 2nd row work 5 rows in rib as for Back. Cast off evenly in rib. Join side seams and armhole borders.

Cicely

Woman's Sweater with Striped Detail (1934)

The perfect garment in which to pine for Errol Flynn. A gem from the thirties that fits perfectly into your eighties wardrobe. The unusual hoops in two contrast shades require care but are not really difficult.

To fit bust		cm	81	86	91	97
(approx)		in	32	34	36	38
Length from top of shoulders		cm	46	47	48	49
(approx)		in	18	18½	19	19½
Sleeve seam		cm	11	11	12	12
(approx)		in	4¼	4¼	4¾	4¾
Patons Beehive 4 ply						
Main colour (A)		50 g balls	5	5	6	6
1st contrast (B)		50 g balls	1	1	1	1
2nd contrast (C)		50 g balls	1	1	1	1

Pair each Nos. 2¾ mm and 3¼ mm needles.
2 buttons.

Tension
On No. 3¼ mm needles, 24 sts and 56 rows to 10 cm (garter stitch).

Abbreviations
K = knit; P = purl; st = stitch; inc = increase; dec = decrease; tog = together; M1 = make a stitch by picking up horizontal loop lying before next stitch and working into back of it; patt = pattern; rep = repeat; cm = centimetres; mm = millimetres; in = inches; A = main shade; B = 1st contrast; C = 2nd contrast.

BACK
With No. 2¾ mm needles and A, cast on 84 [90,96,102] sts and work in K1, P1 rib for 6 cm.
Next row – Rib 3 [6,2,5], M1, rib 6 [6,7,7] 13 times, M1, rib to end. *98 [104,110,116] sts.*

Change to No. 3¼ mm needles and work in patt as follows:
1st row (right side) – In A, K.
2nd to 26th row – In A, K.
27th row – In B, K.
28th row – In B, K10 [11,12,13], (P10, turn, K10, turn, P9, turn, K8, turn, P9, K24 [26,28,30]) twice, P10, turn, K10, turn, P9, turn, K8, turn, P9, K10 [11,12,13].

29th to 54th row – In A, K.
55th row – In C, K.
56th row – In C, K27 [29,31,33], P10, turn, K10, turn, P9, turn, K8, turn, P9, K24 [26,28,30], P10, turn, K10, turn, P9, turn, K8, turn, P9, K27 [29,31,33].
These 56 rows form patt.
Work a further 66 rows in patt, ending with a 10th patt row.
Continue in patt and cast on 22 [22,24,24] sts at beg of next 2 rows for sleeves. *142 [148,158,164] sts.* **
Next 12 rows – In A, K.

Divide for back opening
Next row – In A, K74 [77,82,85], turn and leave remaining sts on a spare needle.
Next row – In A, K.
Next row – In B, K.
Next row – In B, K32 [34,36,38], P10, turn, K10, turn, P9, turn, K8, turn, P9, K to end.
Next 4 rows – In A, K.
Next 2 rows (make 1st buttonhole) – K to last 4 sts, cast off 2 sts, K to end and back, casting on 2 sts above cast-off sts.
Next 10 rows – In A, K.
Next 2 rows – Work 2nd buttonhole as 1st.
Next 5 rows – In A, K.
Next row – In A, cast off 6 sts, K to end. *68 [71,76,79] sts.*

***Next 2 rows – In A, K.
Next row – In C, K.
Next row – In C, K2 tog, K7 [8,9,10], P10, turn, K10, turn, P9, turn, K8, turn, P9, K24 [26,28,30], P10 turn, K10, turn, P9, turn, K8, turn, P9, K15 [15,17,17]. 67 [70,75,78] sts.
Next 26 rows – In A, K; dec 1 st at neck edge on every 4th row. 61 [64,69,72] sts.
Next row – In B, K.
Next row – In B, K2 tog, K17 [19,21,23], P10, turn, K10, turn, P9, turn, K8, turn, P9, K to end. 60 [63,68,71] sts.
Next 24 [26,26,26] rows – In A, K; dec 1 st at neck edge on every 4th row 5 [6,6,6] times, ending with 4 [2,2,2] K rows. 55 [57,62,65] sts.

2nd, 3rd and 4th sizes only
Next row – In C, K.
Next row – In C, K2 tog 0 [1,1] times, K32 [33,36], P10, turn, K10, turn, P9, turn, K8, turn, P9, K15 [17,17]. 57 [61,64] sts.

2nd and 3rd sizes only
K 2 [8] rows in A.

4th size only
K 14 rows in A, dec 1 st at neck edge on 4th row. 63 sts.

All sizes
Cast off. ***

With right side of work facing, rejoin yarn A to remaining sts, cast on 6 sts, K to end. 74 [77,82,85] sts.
Next row – In A, K.
Next row – In B, K.
Next row – In B, K32 [34,36,38], P10, turn, K10, turn, P9, turn, K8, turn, P9, turn, K to end.
Next 22 rows – In A, K.
Next row – In A, cast off 6 sts, K to end. 68 [71,76,79] sts.
Next 3 rows – In A, K.
****Next row – In C, K.
Next row – In C, K15 [15,17,17], P10, turn, K10, turn, P9, turn, K8, turn, P9, K24 [26,28,30], P10, turn, K10, turn, P9, turn, K8, turn, P9, K7 [8,9,10], K2 tog. 67 [70,75,78] sts.
Next 26 rows – In A, K; dec 1 st at neck edge on every 4th row. 61 [64,69,72] sts.
Next row – In B, K.
Next row – In B, K31 [32,35,36], P10, turn, K10, turn, P9, turn, K8, turn, P9, K17 [19,21,23], K2 tog. 60 [63,68,71] sts.
Next 24 [26,26,26] rows – In A, K; dec 1 st at neck

edge on every 4th row 5 [6,6,6] times, ending with 4 [2,2,2] K rows. 55 [57,62,65] sts.

2nd, 3rd and 4th sizes only
Next row – In C, K.
Next row – In C, K15 [17,17,17], P10, turn, K10, turn, P9, turn, K8, turn, P9, K32 [33,36], K2 tog 0 [1,1] times. 57 [61,64] sts.

2nd and 3rd sizes only
K 2 [8] rows in A.

4th size only
K 14 rows in A, dec 1 st at neck edge on 4th row [63 sts].

All sizes
Cast off ****.

FRONT
Work as for Back to **.
Next 14 rows – In A, K.
Next row – In B, K.
Next row – In B, K32 [33,36,37] (P10, turn, K10, turn, P9, turn, K8, turn, P9, K24 [26,28,30]) twice, P10, turn, K10, turn, P9, turn, K8, turn, P9, K32 [33,36,37].
Next 23 rows – In A, K.

Divide for neck as follows:
Next row – In A, K68 [71,76,79], cast off next 6 sts, K to end.
Continue on the first 68 [71,76,79] sts as for Back from *** to ***.
With right side facing and A, rejoin yarn to remaining 68 [71,76,79] sts and K2 rows.
Work as for Back from **** to ****.

SLEEVE BORDERS
With right side facing, No. 2¾ mm needles and A, knit up 70 [74,80,84] sts evenly along sleeve edge.
Work in K1, P1 rib for 2 cm.
Cast off.

COLLAR (make 2)
With No. 3¼ mm needles and A, cast on 122 [126,132,136] sts and K 1 row.
Next row (wrong side) – K1, K2 tog, K to last 3 sts, K2 tog, K1.
Next row – K.
Rep last 2 rows 3 times more.
Next row – K1 (K2 tog, K20 [21,22,23]) twice, K2 tog, K20 [20,22,22], (K2 tog, K20 [21,22,23]) twice, K2 tog, K1.
Next row – K.
Next row – K1, K2 tog, K to last 3 sts, K2 tog, K1.

Next row – K.

Next row – K1, (K2 tog, K18 [19,20,21]) twice, K2 tog, K20 [20,22,22], (K2 tog, K18 [19,20,21]) twice, K2 tog, K1.

Next row – In B, K.

Next row – In B, K1, K2 tog, K7 [7,8,8], (P10, turn, K10, turn, P9, turn, K8, turn, P9, K24 [26,28,30]) twice, P10, turn, K10, turn, P9, turn, K8, turn, P9, K7 [7,8,8], K2 tog, K1.

Break B.

Continue in A.

Next row – K.

Next row – K1 (K2 tog, K16 [17,18,19]) twice, K2 tog, K20 [20,22,22], (K2 tog, K16 [17,18,19]) twice, K2 tog, K1.

Next row – K.

Next row – K1, K2 tog, K to last 3 sts, K2 tog, K1.

Next row – K.

Next row – K1 (K2 tog, K15 [16,17,18]) twice, K2 tog, K16 [16,18,18], (K2 tog, K15 [16,17,18]) twice, K2 tog, K1.

Next row – K.

Next row – K1, K2 tog, K to last 3 sts, K2 tog, K1.

Next row – K.

Next row – K1 (K2 tog, K14 [15,16,17]) twice, K2 tog, K12 [12,14,14], (K2 tog, K14 [15,16,17]) twice, K2 tog, K1.

Next row – K.

Next row – K1, K2 tog, K to last 3 sts, K2 tog, K1.

Next row – K.

Next row – K1 (K2 tog, K12 [13,14,15]) twice, K2 tog, K12 [12,14,14], (K2 tog, K12 [13,14,15]) twice, K2 tog, K1.

Next row – K.

Next row – K1, K2 tog, K to last 3 sts, K1.

Next row – K.

Next row – K1 (K2 tog, K11 [12,13,14]) twice, K2 tog, K8 [8,10,10], (K2 tog, K11 [12,13,14]) twice, K2 tog, K1. *60 [64,70,74] sts.*

Cast off.

TO MAKE UP

Do not press.

Join side and sleeve seams. Place left back part of opening under right back and neatly catch down 6 cast-on sts to wrong side of work.

Sew on buttons to correspond with buttonholes.

Sew cast-off edges of collars to neck edges.

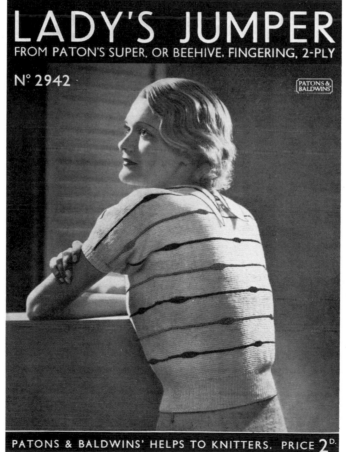

Rosina

Woman's Jumper/Cardigan (1935)

Yesterday's lumber jacket becomes today's bomber jacket. The jumper is designed to pull over your head and button up – or not. Our model wore it with shorts, but it goes equally well with skirts and trousers. The shaped garter-stitch panels make a clever contrast of texture.

To fit bust		cm	86	91	97	102
(approx)	in	34	36	38	40
Approximate length from top of shoulders		cm	51	52	53	54
	in	20	20½	21	21½
Sleeve seam		cm	43	44	44	44
(approx)	in	17	17½	17½	17½
Patons Clansman DK	50 g balls	8	9	9	10

Pair each Nos. 3¼ mm and 4 mm needles.
5 buttons.

Tension

On No. 4 mm needles, 22 sts and 30 rows to 10 cm (stocking stitch), 22 sts and 40 rows to 10 cm (garter stitch).

Abbreviations

K = knit; P = purl; st = stitch; tog = together; inc = increase; dec = decrease; beg = beginning; alt = alternate; rep = repeat; patt = pattern; cm = centimetres; in = inches; mm = millimetres; M1 = make a stitch by picking up horizontal loop lying before next stitch and working into back of it.

FRONT

** With No. 3¼ mm needles cast on 85 [91,97,103] sts and work in rib as follows:
1st row (right side) – K1, *P1, K1; rep from * to end.
2nd row – P1, *K1, P1; rep from * to end.
Rep these 2 rows until work measures 10 cm, ending with a 2nd row.
Next row – Rib 3 [6,5,4], *M1, rib 10 [10,11,12]; rep from * to last 2 [5,4,3] sts, M1, rib to end. 94 [100,106,112] sts. **

Change to No. 4 mm needles and divide for Fronts as follows:
Next row – P35 [38,41,44], K14, turn.
Work on these 49 [52,55,58] sts for left front, leaving remaining sts on spare needle.

Right front

1st row – K.
2nd row – P to last 14 sts, K14.
Rep 1st and 2nd rows 4 times.
11th row – K2, cast off 2, K to last 2 sts, inc in next st, K1.
12th row – P to last 12 sts, K10, cast on 2 sts, K2.
Rep 1st and 2nd rows 10 times.
Rep 11th and 12th rows once.
Rep 1st and 2nd rows 7 times, then 1st row once.
Work garter stitch patt as follows:
1st row (wrong side) – P29 [32,35,38], K1, P7, K14.
2nd and 4th rows – K.
3rd row – P28 [31,34,37], K3, P6, K14.
5th row – P27 [30,33,36], K5, P5, K14.
6th row – K2, cast off 2, K to last 2 sts, inc in next st, K1.
7th row – P27 [30,33,36], K7, P4, K10, cast on 2 sts, K2.
8th and every alt row – K.
9th row – P26 [29,32,35], K9, P3, K14.
11th row – P25 [28,31,34], K11, P2, K14.
13th row – P24 [27,30,33], K13, P1, K14.
15th row – P23 [26,29,32], K29.
17th row – As 15th.
Work 7 rows in garter st (every row K).
Continue in garter st and **shape armhole** by casting off 4 sts at beg of next row.
Dec 1 st at end of next row.
Work 1 row.
Next row – K2, cast off 2, K to last 2 sts, K2 tog.
Next row – K to last 2 sts, cast on 2 sts, K2.

JUMPER-CARDIGAN
FROM PATON'S SUPER, OR BEEHIVE, FINGERING, 4-PLY

No 2322

PATONS & BALDWINS

PATONS & BALDWINS' HELPS TO KNITTERS. PRICE 2^{D.}

Continue to dec 1 st at armhole edge on next and every alt row until 39 [41,42,45] sts remain.
Work 7 [5,1,1] rows.
Next row – K2, cast off 2, K to end.
Next row – K to last 2 sts, cast on 2 sts, K2.

Shape collar as follows:
Next row – K1, inc in next st, K to end.
Work 5 rows.
Rep last 6 rows until there are 47 [50,52,55] sts.
Work 8 [6,4,8] rows, ending with wrong side facing for next row.

Shape shoulder by casting off 7 [7,7,8] sts at beg of next and following alt rows.
Work 1 row.
Cast off 6 [7,7,8] sts at beg of next row, K to end, cast on 13 [15,17,17] sts. *40 [44,48,48] sts.*
Work 12 rows on these sts. Cast off.

Left front
With wrong side of work facing, rejoin yarn to remaining stitches on spare needle, cast on 4 sts, K these sts, then K10, P35 [38,41,44]. *49 [52,55,58] sts.*
1st row – K.
2nd row – K14, P to end.
Rep 1st and 2nd rows 4 times.
Keeping 14 K sts at front edge, inc 1 st at beg of next and following 22nd row.
Work a further 16 rows, ending with wrong side facing for next row.
Work garter st patt as follows:
1st row – K14, P7, K1, P29 [32,35,38].
2nd and 4th rows – K.
3rd row – K14, P6, K3, P28 [31,34,37].
5th row – K14, P5, K5, P27 [30,33,36].
6th row – K1, inc in next st, K to end.
7th row – K14, P4, K7, P27 [30,33,36].
8th and every alt row – K.
9th row – K14, P3, K9, P26 [29,32,35].
11th row – K14, P2, K11, P25 [28,31,34].
13th row – K14, P1, K13, P24 [27,30,33].
15th row – K29, P23 [26,29,32].
17th row – As 15th row.
Work 6 rows in garter st.

Shape armhole by casting off 4 sts at beg of next row.
Work 1 row.
Dec 1 st at beg of next and every alt row until 39 [41,42,45] sts remain.
Work 9 [7,3,3] rows.

Shape collar as follows:
Next row – K to last 3 sts, inc in next st, K2.
Work 5 rows.
Rep last 6 rows until there are 47 [50,52,55] sts.
Work 7 [5,3,7] rows, ending with right side facing for next row.

Shape shoulder by casting off 7 [7,7,8] sts at beg of next and following alt row.
Work 1 row.
Cast off 6 [7,7,8] sts at beg of next row, K to end.
K 1 row.
Next row – K27 [29,31,31], cast on 13 [15,17,17] sts. *40 [44,48,48] sts.*
Work 12 rows on these sts. Cast off.

BACK
Work as for Front from ** to **.

Change to No. 4 mm needles and P 1 row.
Starting with a K row, work in stocking st, shaping sides by inc 1 st at each end of 11th and every following 22nd row until there are 100 [106,112,118] sts.
Work a further 12 rows. Continue now in garter st and work 5 rows.

Shape armholes by casting off 4 sts at beg of next 2 rows.
Dec 1 st at each end of next and every alt row until 74 [78,80,86] sts remain.
Work straight until Back measures same as Front to start of shoulder shaping, ending with right side facing for next row.

Shape shoulders by casting off 7 [7,7,8] sts at beg of next 4 rows, then 6 [7,7,8] sts at beg of following 2 rows.
Cast off remaining 34 [36,38,38] sts.

SLEEVES
With No. 3¼ mm needles, cast on 43 [45,47,47] sts and work 10 cm in rib as for Front, ending with a 1st row.
Next row – Rib 4 [5,6,6], * M1, rib 5 [4,4,4]; rep from * to last 4 [4,5,5] sts, M1, rib to end. *51 [55,57,57] sts.*

Change to No. 4 mm needles and, starting with a K row, work in stocking st, shaping sides by inc 1 st at each end of 5th [7th,7th,9th] and every following 10th [10th,10th,8th] row until there are 71 [75,77,81] sts.

Work straight until sleeve seam measures 17 [17½,17½,17½] cm, ending with a P row.

Shape top by casting off 4 sts at beg of next 2 rows.
Dec 1 st at each end of next and every following 4th row until 55 [59,61,65] sts remain.
Work 1 row.
Dec 1 st at each end of next and every alt row until 29 sts remain. Work 1 row.
Dec 1 st at each end of every row until 21 sts remain.
Cast off.

TO MAKE UP
Press, following instructions on yarn label.
Join shoulder seams; then join the bands from fronts to form the collar and sew to back of neck.
Join side and sleeve seams. Insert sleeves.
Sew the 4 cast-on sts at base of front opening in position on wrong side of fabric.
Sew on buttons.
Fold collar to right side.
Press seams.

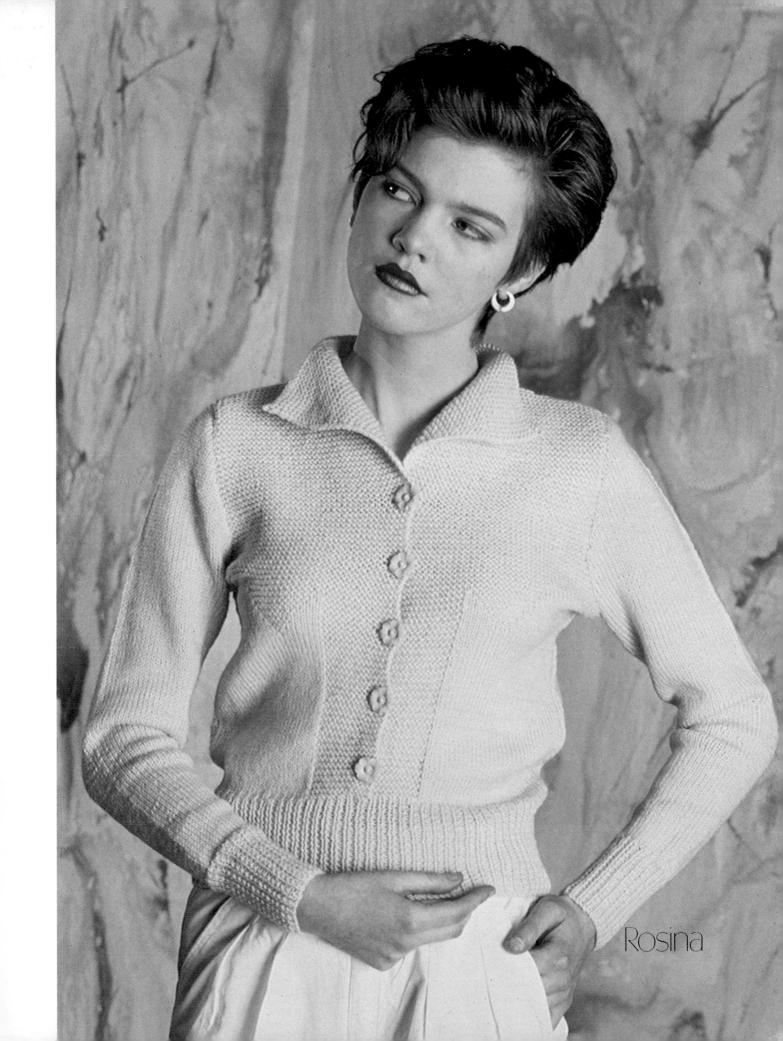

Rosina

Cicely

Leonard

Lilian

Leonard

Man's Cable and Moss-stitch Pullover (1935)

A chunky knit with an unusual cable pattern that flatters the man beneath. Once you've mastered the basic cable pattern your needles will fly.

			97	102	107
To fit chest		cm	97	102	107
	(approx)	in	38	40	42
Length from top of shoulders		cm	57	58	59
	(approx)	in	22½	23	23½
Patons Moorland Shetland Chunky	50 g balls		8	9	10

Pair each Nos. 5 mm and 6 mm needles.
Cable needle.

Tension
On No. 6 mm needles 15 sts and 20 rows to 10 cm (moss stitch).

Abbreviations
K = knit; P = purl; st = stitch; tog = together; tbl = through back of loop; dec = decrease; M1 = make a stitch by picking up horizontal loop lying before next stitch and working into the back of it; patt = pattern; alt = alternate; beg = beginning; cm = centimetres; mm = millimetres; in = inches; C6B = slip next 3 sts on cable needle to back of work, K3, then K3 from cable needle; C6F = slip next 3 sts on cable needle to front of work, K3, then K3 from cable needle.

Panel patt (12 sts)
1st row (Right side) – K.
2nd row – P.
3rd and 4th rows – As 1st and 2nd.
5th row – C6B, C6F.
6th row – P.
7th and 8th rows – As 1st and 2nd.

BACK
With No. 5 mm needles, cast on 66 [70,74] sts and work in K1, P1 rib for 6 cm.
Next row – Rib 1 [2,4], M1, rib 2 [3,3], M1, (rib 3, M1) 20 times, rib 2 [3,3], M1, rib 1 [2,4]. *89 [93,97] sts.*

Change to No. 6 mm needles and work in patt as follows:
1st row (Right side) – (P1, K1) 6 [7,7] times, P1, panel patt 12 as 1st row, (P1, K1) 1 [1,2] times, P1, panel patt 12 as 1st row, (P1, K1) 4 times, P1, panel patt 12 as 1st row, (P1, K1) 1 [1,2] times, P1, panel patt 12 as 1st row, (P1, K1) 6 [7,7] times, P1.
2nd row – (P1, K1) 6 [7,7] times, P1, panel patt 12 as 2nd row, (P1, K1) 1 [1,2] times, P1, panel patt 12 as 2nd row, (P1, K1) 4 times, P1, panel patt 12 as 2nd row, (P1, K1) 1 [1,2] times, P1, panel patt 12 as 2nd row, (P1, K1) 6 [7,7] times, P1.
Continue in patt thus, working appropriate rows of panel patt, until Back measures 34 cm, ending with right side facing for next row.**

Keeping patt correct, **shape armholes** by casting off 4 sts at beg of next 2 rows, then dec 1 st at each end of following 3 rows.
Work 1 row.
Dec 1 st at each end of next and 1 [2,2] following alt rows. *71 [73,77] sts.*
Work straight in patt until Back measures 57 [58,59] cm, ending with wrong side facing for next row.
Next row – Patt 4 [5,5], (P1, P2 tog) 4 times, patt 3 [3,5], (P1, P2 tog) 3 times, patt 15, (P2 tog, P1) 3 times, patt 3 [3,5], (P2 tog, P1) 4 times, patt 4 [5,5]. *57 [59,63] sts.*

Shape shoulder as follows:
Next row – Cast off 5 sts (1 st on right needle), K6 [7,7], (P1, K1) 16 [16,18] times, P1, K8, (P1, K1) twice, P0 [1,1].
Next row – Cast off 5 sts (1 st on right needle), P6 [7,7], (P1, K1) 16 [16,18] times, P8 [9,9].

Keeping patt as set, cast off 5 [5,6] at beg of next 4 rows.
Cast off remaining 27 [29,29] sts.

FRONT
Work as for Back to **.

Keeping patt correct, **shape armhole** by casting off 4 sts at beg of next 2 rows.

Continue shaping armholes and divide for neck as follows:
1st row – Work 2 tog, patt 32 [34,36], K2 tog, (P1, K1) twice, turn and leave remaining sts on a spare needle.
Continue on these 38 [40,42] sts for first side as follows:
2nd row – (K1, P1) twice, patt to last 2 sts, work 2 tog.
3rd row – Work 2 tog, patt to last 6 sts, K2 tog, (P1, K1) twice.
4th row – (K1, P1) twice, patt to end.
Rep 3rd and 4th rows 2 [3,3] times more. *31 [31,33] sts.*
Next row – Patt to last 4 sts, (P1, K1) twice.
Next row – (K1, P1) twice, P2 tog, patt to end.
Next row – Patt to last 4 sts, (P1, K1) twice.
Next row – (K1, P1) twice, patt to end.
Next row – Patt to last 6 sts, K2 tog, (P1, K1) twice.
Next row – (K1, P1) twice, patt to end.
Rep last 6 rows until 19 [19,21] sts remain. Work a few rows straight if necessary until Front matches Back at armhole edge. End with wrong side facing for next row.
Next row – Patt 3 [2,4], (P2 tog, P1) 4 times, (P1, K1) twice, P0 [1,1]. *15 [15,17] sts.*

Shape shoulder by casting off 5 sts at beg of next row, then 5 [5,6] sts at beg of 2 following alt rows.
With right side facing, rejoin yarn to remaining sts, cast off 1 [1 st on right needle], P1, K1, P1, K2 tog tbl, patt to last 2 sts, work 2 tog. *38 [40,42] sts.*
2nd row – Work 2 tog, patt to last 4 sts, (P1, K1) twice.
3rd row – (K1, P1) twice, K2 tog tbl, patt to last 2 sts, work 2 tog.
4th row – Patt to last 4 sts, (P1, K1) twice.
Rep 3rd and 4th rows 2 (3,3) times more. *31 [31,33] sts.*
Next row – (K1, P1) twice, patt to end.
Next row – Patt to last 6 sts, P2 tog tbl, (P1, K1) twice.
Next row – (K1, P1) twice, patt to end.
Next row – Patt to last 4 sts, (P1, K1) twice.
Next row – (K1, P1) twice, K2 tog tbl, patt to end.
Next row – Patt to last 4 sts, (P1, K1) twice.
Rep last 6 rows until 19 [19,21] sts remain. Work a few rows straight if necessary until Front matches Back at armhole edge. End with wrong side facing for next row.
Next row – P0 [1,1], (K1, P1) twice, (P1, P2 tog) 4 times, patt 3 [2,4]. *15 [15,17] sts.* Work 1 row.

Shape shoulder by casting off 5 sts at beg of next row, then 5 [5,6] sts at beg of 2 following alternate rows.

TO MAKE UP
Omitting ribbing, press parts lightly on wrong side, following instructions on yarn label and taking care not to spoil the pattern.
Join shoulder and side seams and press seams lightly.

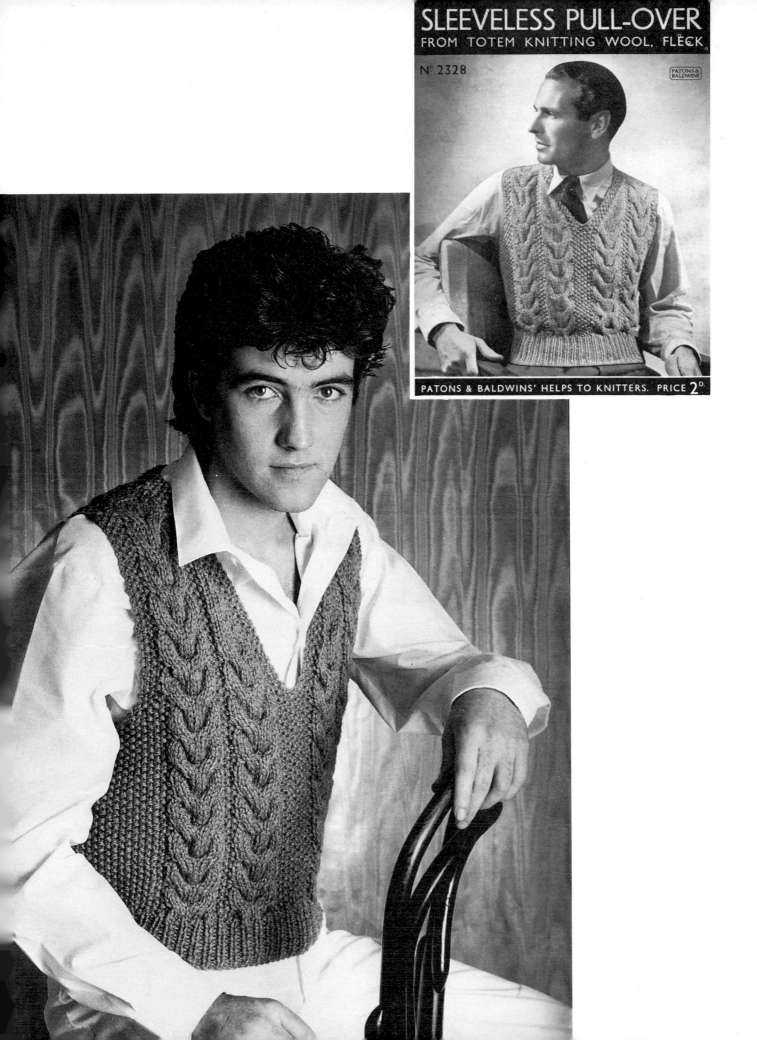

SLEEVELESS PULL-OVER
FROM TOTEM KNITTING WOOL, FLECK.

Nº 2328

PATONS & BALDWINS

PATONS & BALDWINS' HELPS TO KNITTERS. PRICE 2ᴰ.

 Sheila

Woman's Stripe-patterned Crossover Cardigan (1936)

A classic from the late thirties, when style really mattered. Wonderfully elegant, it is made entirely in garter stitch; you could use subtle pastels or bold contrasting colours as we have. A look at the picture shows how to fold the unusual crossover front.

To fit bust		cm	81–6	89–94
	(approx)	in	32–4	35–7
Approximate length from top of shoulders		cm	55	56
		in	21½	22
Approximate sleeve seam		cm	14	14
		in	5½	5½
Patons Clansman 4 ply				
Main shade (A)		50 g balls	4	5
1st contrast (B)		50 g balls	1	1
2nd contrast (C)		50 g balls	1	1

Pair No. 3¼ mm needles.
1 press-stud.

Tension
On No. 3¼ mm needles, 24 sts and 48 rows to 10 cm (over patt).

Abbreviations
K = knit; P = purl; sts = stitches; tog = together; patt = pattern; rep = repeat; M1 = make a stitch by picking up horizontal loop lying before next stitch and working into back of it; mm = millimetres; in = inches; cm = centimetres; A = main shade; B = 1st contrast; C = 2nd contrast.

Stripe patt
1st row (right side) – In A, K.
2nd to 6th rows – As 1st.
7th row – In B, K.
8th row – In B, P.
9th to 14th rows – As 1st to 6th.
15th row – In C, K.
16th row – In C, P.
These 16 rows form patt.

BACK
With A, cast on 84 sts and, starting with 1st row of stripe patt, work as follows:

1st row (right side) – Patt 3, turn.
2nd row – Patt to end.
3rd and 4th rows – Patt 5, turn and patt to end.
5th and 6th rows – Patt 8, turn and patt to end.
7th and 8th rows – Patt 10, turn and patt to end.
9th and 10th rows – Patt 13, turn and patt to end.
11th and 12th rows – Patt 15, turn and patt to end.
13th and 14th rows – Patt 18, turn and patt to end.
15th and 16th rows – Patt 20, turn and patt to end.
Starting with 1st row of patt, continue as follows:
17th row – Patt to end.
18th and 19th rows – Patt 13, turn and patt to end.
20th and 21st rows – Patt 18, turn and patt to end.
22nd and 23rd rows – Patt 23, turn and patt to end.
24th and 25th rows – Patt 28, turn and patt to end.
26th and 27th rows – Patt 33, turn and patt to last st, M1, patt 1.
28th and 29th rows – Patt 39, turn and patt to last st, M1, patt 1.
30th and 31st rows – Patt 45, turn and patt to last st, M1, patt 1.
32nd and 33rd rows – Patt 51, turn and patt to last st, M1, patt 1.
34th row – Patt 1, M1 [0], patt to end. *89 [88] sts.*
35th row – Patt to last st, M1, patt 1.
36th row – Patt 1, M1 [0], patt to end.
37th row – Patt to last st, M1, patt 1.
38th row – Patt 1, M1, patt to end.

...

Nº 3474
JUMPER

PATON'S SUPER, or BEEHIVE,
SCOTCH FINGERING, 2-PLY

PRICE **3**D.
This price only applies
in Great Britain and
Northern Ireland

PATONS &
BALDWINS

A "P&B" PUBLICATION

Rep last 2 rows 3 [4] times more. *99 sts.*
Next row – Patt to end, cast on 27 [31] sts. *126 [130] sts.*

Continue for left shoulder as follows:
Patt 3 [7] rows.
Next row – Patt to last st, M1, patt 1.
Patt 7 rows.
Rep last 8 rows 5 times more. *132 [136] sts.*
Patt 36 [40] rows.

Continue for right shoulder as follows:
Next row – Patt 1, work 2 tog, patt to end.
Patt 7 rows.
Rep last 8 rows 4 times more.
Next row – Patt 1, work 2 tog, patt to end.
Work 4 [8] rows in patt. *126 [130] sts.*
Next row – Cast off 27 [31] sts, patt to end. *99 sts.*
Next row – Patt to last 3 sts, work 2 tog, patt 1.
Next row – Patt 1, work 2 tog, patt to end.
Rep last 2 rows 4 times. *89 sts.*

1st size only
Next row – Patt to last 3 sts, work 2 tog, patt 1. *88 sts.*

2nd size only
Next row – Patt to end.
Next row – Patt 1, work 2 tog, patt to end. *88 sts.*
Next row – Patt to end.

Both sizes
Next 2 rows – Patt 1, work 2 tog, patt 49, turn and patt to end.
Next 2 rows – Patt 1, work 2 tog, patt 43, turn and patt to end.
Next 2 rows – Patt 1, work 2 tog, patt 37, turn and patt to end.
Next 2 rows – Patt 1, work 2 tog, patt 31, turn and patt to end.
Next 2 rows – Patt 28, turn and patt to end.
Next 2 rows – Patt 23, turn and patt to end.
Next 2 rows – Patt 18, turn and patt to end.
Next 2 rows – Patt 13, turn and patt to end.
Next row – Patt to end. *84 sts.*
Last row was a 14th row of patt.
Starting with 15th row of patt, continue as follows:
Next 2 rows – Patt 20, turn and patt to end.
Next 2 rows – Patt 18, turn and patt to end.
Next 2 rows – Patt 15, turn and patt to end.
Next 2 rows – Patt 13, turn and patt to end.
Next 2 rows – Patt 10, turn and patt to end.
Next 2 rows – Patt 8, turn and patt to end.
Next 2 rows – Patt 5, turn and patt to end.
Next 2 rows – Patt 3, turn and patt to end.
Cast off all sts.

LEFT FRONT
** With A, cast on 136 [140] sts and, starting with 1st row of stripe patt, work 4 [8] rows.

Shape shoulder as follows:
Next row – Patt to last st, M1, patt 1.
Patt 7 rows.
Rep last 8 rows 4 times more.
Next row – Patt to last st, M1, patt 1. *142 [146] sts.***
Next row – In patt.
*** **Next 2 rows** – Patt to last 2 [3] sts, turn and patt to end.
Next 2 rows – Patt to last 4 [6] sts, turn and patt to end.
Next 2 rows – Patt to last 6 [8] sts, turn and patt to end.
Next 2 rows – Patt to last 8 [10] sts, turn and patt to end.
Next 2 rows – Patt to last 10 [12] sts, turn and patt to end.
Next 2 rows – Patt to last 12 [14] sts, turn and patt to end.
Next 2 rows – Patt to last 14 [16] sts, turn and patt to end.
Next 2 rows – Patt to last 16 [18] sts, turn and patt to end.
Next 2 rows – Patt to last 18 [20] sts, turn and patt to end.
Next 2 rows – Patt to last 20 [22] sts, turn and patt to end.
Next 2 rows – Patt to last 22 [24] sts, turn and patt to end.
Next 2 rows – Patt to last 24 [26] sts, turn and patt to end.
Next 2 rows – Patt to last 25 [28] sts, turn and patt to end.
Next 2 rows – Patt to last 26 [30] sts, turn and patt to end.***
Next 2 rows – Cast off 56 sts, patt to last 27 [31] sts, turn and patt to end.
Next row – Cast on 44 sts, patt these 44 sts, then patt to last 27 [31] sts, cast off these 27 [31] sts loosely. *103 sts.*
Break yarn. With wrong side facing, rejoin appropriate yarn to remaining sts and patt to end.
****Patt 1 [3] rows.
Next row – Patt 1, work 2 tog, patt to end.
Patt 4 rows.
Next row – Patt 1, work 2 tog, patt to last 3 sts, work 2 tog, patt 1.
Rep last 5 rows 4 times more. *92 sts.*
Patt 1 row.

Next row – Patt to last st, M1, patt 1.
Patt 1 row.
Next row – Patt to last st, M1, patt 1.
Next row – Patt to last 3 sts, work 2 tog, patt 1.
Next row – Patt to last st, M1, patt 1.
Patt 1 row.
Rep last 2 rows again.
Next row – Patt 1, work 2 tog, patt to last st, M1, patt 1.
Patt 1 row.
Next 2 rows – Patt to last 5 sts, turn and patt to end.
Next 2 rows – Patt to last 8 sts, turn and patt to last 3 sts, work 2 tog, patt 1.
Next 2 rows – Patt to last 11 sts, turn and patt to end.
Next 2 rows – Patt to last 15 sts, turn and patt to end.
Next 2 rows – Patt 1, work 2 tog, patt to last 19 sts, turn and patt to end.
Next 2 rows – Patt to last 23 sts, turn and patt to end.
Next 2 rows – Patt to last 27 sts, turn and patt to last 3 sts, work 2 tog, patt 1.
Next 2 rows – Patt to last 31 sts, turn and patt to end.
Next 2 rows – Patt to last 35 sts, turn and patt to end.
Next 2 rows – Patt 1, work 2 tog, patt to last 39 sts, turn and patt to end.
Next 2 rows – Patt to last 43 sts, turn and patt to end.
Next 2 rows – Patt to last 47 sts, turn and patt to last 3 sts, work 2 tog, patt 1.
Next row – Patt 23, cast off remaining 67 sts loosely.
Patt 1 row.
Next row – Patt to last 3 sts, work 2 tog, patt 1.
Patt 1 row.
Next row – Patt 1, work 2 tog, patt to last 3 sts, work 2 tog, patt 1.
Patt 1 row.
Next row – Patt to last 3 sts, work 2 tog, patt 1.
Patt 1 row.
Next row – Patt to last 3 sts, work 2 tog, patt 1.
Next row – Patt to last 3 sts, work 2 tog, patt 1.
Next row – Patt to last 3 sts, work 2 tog, patt 1.
Rep last 10 rows again. *9 sts.*
Patt 1 row.
Next row – Patt 6, work 2 tog, patt 1.
Patt 1 row.
Next row – Patt 1, work 2 tog, patt 2, work 2 tog, patt 1.
Patt 1 row.

Next row – Patt 3, work 2 tog, patt 1.
Patt 1 row.
Next row – Work 2 tog, patt 1, work 2 tog.
Next row – Work 3 tog and fasten off.

RIGHT FRONT
Work as for Left Front from **, but reversing shoulder shapings, thus inc at *beg* of row in place of *end* of row.
Now work as for Left Front from *** to ***.
Next 2 rows – Cast off 12 sts, patt to last 27 [31] sts, turn and patt to end.
Next row – Patt to last 27 [31] sts, cast off these 27 [31] sts loosely. *103 sts.*
Break yarn. With right side facing, rejoin appropriate yarn to remaining sts and patt to end.
Work as for Left Front from **** to end.

SLEEVES
With A, cast on 30 sts and work as follows:
1st row – K.
2nd and 3rd rows – K4, turn and K to end and cast on 1 st.
4th and 5th rows – K9, turn and K to end and cast on 1 st.
6th and 7th rows – K14, turn and K to end and cast on 1 st.
8th and 9th rows – K19, turn and K to end and cast on 1 st.
10th and 11th rows – K24, turn and K to end and cast on 1 st.
12th and 13th rows – K29, turn and K to end and cast on 1 [2] sts.
14th row – K.
Continue in stripe patt starting with a 7th [5th] row and continue as follows:
15th row – Patt to end, cast on 1 st.
16th row – In patt.
17th row – Patt to end, cast on 2 sts.
18th row – In patt.
Rep 15th to 18th rows 7 times more, then 15th row again. *61 [62] sts.*
Note that the last row was a 7th [5th] row of stripe patt.
Continue straight in stripe patt for 48 [52] rows.
Next row – Cast off 1 st, patt to end.
Patt 1 row.
Next row – Cast off 2 sts, patt to end.
Patt 1 row.
Rep last 4 rows 7 times more. *37 [38] sts.*
Next row – Cast off 1 st, patt to end.
Patt 1 row.
Continue in A only as follows:

Next 2 rows – Cast off 1 [2] sts, K to last 6 sts, turn and K to end.
Next 2 rows – Cast off 1 st, K to last 10 sts, turn and K to end.
Next 2 rows – Cast off 1 st, K to last 14 sts, turn and K to end.
Next 2 rows – Cast off 1 st, K to last 18 sts, turn and K to end.
Next 2 rows – Cast off 1 st, K to last 22 sts, turn and K to end.
Next 2 rows – Cast off 1 st, K to last 26 sts, turn and K to end.
Cast off remaining 30 sts.

CUFFS
With right side of sleeve facing and A, knit up 59 [61] sts along straight sleeve edge. Work 6 cm in garter stitch, ending with wrong side facing for next row. Cast off.

TO MAKE UP
Press parts very lightly on wrong side, following instructions on yarn bands.
Join shoulder, side and sleeve seams; insert sleeves.
Sew press-stud in position at the lower edge to fasten the two fronts together.

Lilian

Woman's Sweater with Coloured Squares (1937)

This was originally intended for teenagers, but we've adapted it to fit larger sizes as well. Its jaunty design looks well in any number of colour permutations, so you can go to town with all your odds and ends of double-knit yarn if you feel so inclined.

To fit bust		cm	76	81	86	91	97
	(approx)	in	30	32	34	36	38
Length from top of shoulders		cm	51	52	54	55	56
	(approx)	in	20	20½	21	21½	22
Sleeve seam		cm	8	8	9	9	9
	(approx)	in	3	3	3½	3½	3½
Patons Beehive (knits as 4 ply)							
Main shade (A)	50 g balls		4	4	5	5	5
1st contrast (B)	50 g balls		1	1	1	1	1
2nd contrast (C)	50 g balls		1	1	1	1	1

Pair each Nos. 2¾ mm and 3¼ mm needles.

Tension

On No. 3¼ mm needles 28 sts and 36 rows to 10 cm (stocking st).

Abbreviations

K = knit; P = purl; st = stitch; tog = together; inc = increase; dec = decrease; patt = pattern; beg = beginning; rep = repeat, alt = alternate; cm = centimetres; mm = millimetres; in = inches; A = main shade; B = 1st contrast shade; C = 2nd contrast shade.

Note

When working coloured squares, do not carry yarns across back of work but divide yarns into separate balls as required. Twist yarns on wrong side when changing colours to avoid making a hole.

BACK

With No. 2¾ mm needles and A, cast on 100 [106,112,118,126] sts and work in K1, P1 rib for 9 [9,10,10,10] cm, inc 8 [8,10, 10, 10] sts evenly on last row. *108 [114, 122, 128, 136] sts.*

Change to No. 3¼ mm needles and work in patt as follows:

1st row – In A, K.

2nd row – In A, P.

3rd to 12th rows – Rep 1st and 2nd rows 5 times.

13th row – K14 [15,16,17,19] A, (8 [8,10,10,10] B, 28 [30,30,32,34] A) twice, 8 [8,10,10,10] B, 14 [15,16,17,19] A.

14th row – P14 [15,16,17,19] A, (8 [8,10,10,10] B, 28 [30,30,32,34] A) twice, 8 [8,10,10,10] B, 14 [15,16,17,19] A.

15th to 20th rows – Rep 13th and 14th rows 3 times.

21st to 32nd row – As 1st to 12th.

33rd row – K4 [4,6,6,7] C, (28 [30,30,32,34] A, 8 [8,10,10,10] C) twice, 28 [30,30,32,34] A, 4 [4,6,6,7] C.

34th row – P4 [4,6,6,7] C, (28 [30,30,32,34] A, 8 [8,10,10,10] C) twice, 28 [30,30,32,34] A, 4 [4,6,6,7] C.

35th to 40th row – Rep 33rd row and 34th row 3 times more.

These 40 rows form the patt.

Continue in patt until Back measures approx 34 [34,35,35,35] cm, ending with 12th row of patt.

Keeping patt correct, **shape armhole** by casting off 4 sts at beg of next 2 rows, then dec 1 st at each end of following 5 [5,7,7,9] rows. Work 1 row. Now dec 1 st at each end of next and 2 [3,3,4,3] following alt rows. *84 [88,92,96,102] sts*

5th size only
Next row – In A, P.

Next row – In A, K2 tog, K to last 2 sts, K2 tog. *100 sts.*

All sizes
Continue in A only and work 4 [6,6,8,8] rows straight.
Next row – P across row, inc 5 sts evenly. *89 [93,97,101,105] sts.*
Next row – K1, *P1, K1; rep from * to end.
Next row – P1, *K1, P1; rep from * to end.
Rep last 2 rows until work measures 14 [15,16,17,18] cm from cast-off sts at armhole, ending with right side facing for next row.

Divide for neck as follows:
*** **Next row** – Rib 25 [25,27,27,29], cast off next 39 [43,43,47,47] sts, then rib remaining 25 [25,27,27,29] sts (including st on needle after casting off).
Continue on the first 25 [25,27,27,29] sts as follows:
Next row – P1, *K1, P1; rep from * to last 2 sts, K2.
Next row – K1, *P1, K1; rep from * to end.
Rep last 2 rows until work measures 17 [18,19,20,21] cm from cast-off armhole sts, ending with wrong side facing for next row.

Shape shoulders by casting off 9 sts at beg of next row, then 8 [8,9,9,10] sts at beg of 2 following alt rows.

With wrong side facing, rejoin yarn to remaining 25 [25,27,27,29] sts and work as follows:
Next row – K2, P1, *K1, P1; rep from * to end.
Next row – K1, *P1, K1; rep from * to end.
Rep last 2 rows until work measures 17 [18,19,20,21] cm from cast-off sts at armhole, ending with right side facing for next row.
Shape shoulders as for other side.

FRONT
Work as for Back until work measures 11 [12,12,13,14] cm from cast-off sts at armholes, ending with right side facing for next row.
Complete as for Back from *** to end.

SLEEVES
With No. 2¼ mm needles and A, cast on 68 [70,72,74,78] sts and work 3 [3,4,4,4] cm in K1, P1 rib, inc 10 [10,12,12,12] sts evenly on last row. *78 [80,84,86,90] sts.*

Change to No. 3¼ mm needles and, starting with a K row, work 4 rows in stocking st.
Next row – K7 [6,7,6,6] C, 28 [30,30,32,34] A, 8 [8,10,10,10] C, 28 [30,30,32,34] A, 7 [6,7,6,6,] C.
Next row – P7 [6,7,6,6] C, 28 [30,30,32,34] A, 8 [8, 10,10,10] C, 28 [30,30,32,34] A, 7 [6,7,6,6] C.

Rep last 2 rows 3 times more.
Work 8 rows in A.
Continue in A. **Shape top** by casting off 4 sts at beg of next 2 rows, then dec 1 st at each end of following row. Work 1 row.
Next row – K2 tog in A, K10 [10,10,10,11] A, 8 [8,10,10,10] B, 28 [30,30,32,34] A, 8 [8,10,10,10] B, 10 [10,10,10,11] A, K2 tog in A.
Next row – P11 [11,11,11,12] A, 8 [8,10,10,10] B, 28 [30,30,32,34] A, 8 [8,10,10,10] B, 11 [11,11,11,12] A.
Next row – K2 tog in A, K9 [9,9,9,10] A, 8 [8,10,10,10] B, 28 [30,30,32,34] A, 8 [8,10,10,10] B, 9 [9,9,9,10] A, K2 tog in A.
Next row – P10 [10,10,10,11] A, 8 [8,10,10,10] B, 28 [30,30,32,34] A, 8 [8,10,10,10] B, 10 [10,10,10,11] A.
Next row – K2 tog in A, K8 [8,8,8,9] A, 8 [8,10,10,10] B, 28 [30,30,32,34] A, 8 [8,10,10,10] B, 8 [8,8,8,9] A, K2 tog in A.
Next row – P9 [9,9,9,10] A, 8 [8,10,10,10] B, 28 [30,30,32,34] A, 8 [8,10,10,10] B, 9 [9,9,9,10] A.
Next row – K2 tog in A, K7 [7,7,7,8] A, 8 [8,10,10,10] B, 28 [30,30,32,34] A, 8 [8,10,10,10] B, 7 [7,7,7,8] A, K2 tog in A.
Next row – P8 [8,8,8,9] A, 8 [8,10,10,10] B, 28 [30,30,32,34] A, 8 [8,10,10,10] B, 8 [8,8,8,9] A.
Continue in A only and dec 1 st at each end of next and 5 following alt rows. Work 1 row. *48 [50,54,56,60] sts.*
Next row – K2 tog in A, K18 [19,20,21,23] A, 8 [8,10,10,10] C, 18 [19,20,21,23] A, K2 tog in A.
Next row – P19 [20,21,22,24] A, 8 [8,10,10,10] C, P19 [20,21,22,24] A.
Next row – K2 tog in A, K17 [18,19,20,22] A, 8 [8,10,10,10] C, 17 [18,19,20,22] A, K2 tog in A.
Next row – P18 [19,20,21,23] A, 8 [8,10,10,10] C, 18 [19,20,21,23] A.
Next row – K2 tog in A, K16 [17,18,19,21] A, 8 [8,10,10,10] C, 16 [17,18,19,21] A, K2 tog in A.
Next row – P17 [18,19,20,22] A, 8 [8,10,10,10] C, 17 [18,19,20,22] A.
Next row – K2 tog in A, K15 [16,17,18,20] A, 8 [8,10,10,10] C, 15 [16,17,18,20] A, K2 tog in A.
Next row – P16 [17,18,19,21] A, 8 [8,10,10,10] C, 16 [17,18,19,21] A. Continue in A only and dec 1 st at each end of next and every following alt row until 26 [26,28,28,28] sts remain.
Cast off.

TO MAKE UP
Do not press.
Join shoulder, side and sleeve seams; insert sleeves.

PRICE
2 D.

GIRL'S JUMPER
FROM SUPER OR BEEHIVE FINGERING 3-PLY

Faith

Woman's Hat with Seam Detail (1937)

Materials
1 50 g ball Patons Moorland Tweed or Shetland DK.
Pair No. 4 mm needles.
3 buttons or a decorative pin.

Measurements
To fit average woman's head.

Tension
On 4 mm needles, 20 sts and 40 rows to 10 cm
(garter stitch).

Abbreviations
K = knit; st = stitch; tog = together; inc =
increase; cm = centimetres; in = inches; mm =
millimetres.

HAT
Cast on 57 sts.

We've taken the buttons away and spiked the zany hat with a chopstick. Although there are thirteen years between the two designs, we knitted the hat in thick shetland wool to match the scarf on p. 20.

1st row – K1, K2 tog, K to last 2 sts, inc in next st, K1.
2nd row – K.
Rep last 2 rows until work measures 48 cm, ending with a 1st row.
Cast off.

TO MAKE UP
Join cast-on and cast-off edges.
Fold hat so that seam starts at lower left-hand corner and slopes across the front.
Sew buttons or decorative pin into position. If using buttons, the first should be 1 cm from left edge of hat and 1 cm up from lower edge, the second 4 cm from edge and 6 cm up from lower edge; the third 7 cm from edge and 11 cm up from lower edge, sewing through double thickness of hat. Stitch through both layers from top button, sloping up to 1 cm from top of the hat, then curving round to the opposite edge 9 cm from the top.

PATONS & BALDWINS' HELPS TO KNITTERS 2/472

PRICE 2ᴰ·

WOOL HATS
FROM 3-PLY "WOODPECKER" YARN

Woman's Jumper (1937)

Horizontal and vertical contrasts make this neat little jersey fun to knit and fun to wear. Make the contrasts as daring as you like, and add a belt if you feel like it.

		81	86	91	97
To fit bust	cm	81	86	91	97
(approx)	in	32	34	36	38
Approximate length from top of shoulders	cm	55	56	57	58
	in	21½	22	22½	23
Approximate sleeve seam	cm	20	20	20	20
	in	8	8	8	8
Patons Beehive (knits as 4 ply)					
Main shade (A)	50 g balls	6	6	7	7
Contrast (B)	50 g balls	6	6	7	7

Pair No. 3¼ mm needles.
5 buttons.

Tension
On No. 3¼ mm needles, 24 sts and 56 rows to 10 cm (garter st).

Abbreviations
K = knit; P = purl; st = stitch; tog = together; dec = decrease; inc = increase; beg = beginning; patt = pattern; rep = repeat; alt = alternate; cm = centimetres; in = inches; mm = millimetres; A = main shade; B = contrast shade.

LEFT BACK
With A, cast on 43 [46,49,52] sts and work in patt as follows:
1st row (right side) – In A, K.
2nd row – In A, K.
3rd and 4th rows – In B, K.
These 4 rows form patt; garment is worked in patt throughout.
Continue in patt until work measures 19 cm, ending with right side facing for next row.

Shape side edge by inc 1 st at end of next and every following 14th row, until there are 49 [52,55,58] sts. Work straight until Back measures 37 cm, ending with wrong side facing for next row.

Shape armhole by casting off 3 sts at beg of next row, then dec 1 st at armhole edge on following 3 [5,5,7] rows.

Work 1 row.
Now dec 1 st at armhole edge on next and following 3 [3,4,4] alt rows. *39 [40,42,43] sts.* **
Work straight until Back measures 41 [42,43,44] cm, ending with right side facing for next row.
Next row – Cast on 2 sts, K these 2 sts, K to end. *41 [42,44,45] sts.*
Work straight until Back measures 55 [56,57,58] cm, ending with wrong side facing for next row.

Shape shoulder by casting off 5 [5,6,6] sts at beg of next row, then 6 sts at beg of following 3 alt rows. Cast off remaining 18 [19,20,21] sts.

RIGHT FRONT
Work as for Left Back to **.
Work straight until Front measures 49 [50,51, 52] cm, ending with right side facing for next row.

Shape neck as follows:
Next row – Cast off 8 [9,10,11] sts, K to end.
Dec 1 st at neck edge on next 4 rows. Work 1 row.
Now dec 1 st at neck edge on next and following 3 alt rows. *23 [23, 24,24] sts.*
Work straight until Front measures 55 [56,57,58] cm, ending with wrong side facing for next row.

Shape shoulder by casting off 5 [5,6,6] sts at beg of next row, then 6 sts at beg of following 3 alt rows.

RIGHT BACK
With A, cast on 37 sts and work 4 rows in stripe patt.
Make buttonholes in next 2 rows as follows:

Freda

Sheila

Faith

Ronald and Rona

Next row – Cast on 97 [100,102,104] sts, K these 97 [100,102,104] sts, (K5, cast off 2) 5 times, K2.
Next row – K2, (cast on 2, K5) 5 times, K to end. *134 [137,139,141] sts.*
Work 34 [37,39,42] rows.
Place a marker at beg [end, end, beg] of last row.
This denotes end of back neck. Work 13 rows.
Dec 1 st at beg [end,end,beg] of next row and at the same edge on 2 following 14th rows. *131 [134,136,138] sts.*
Work 11 [12,14,15] rows.

Shape armhole by casting off 36 [38,40,41] sts at beg of next row. Now dec 1 st at end of next and following 3 [3,2,2] alt rows. Work 1 [3,3,3] rows.

2nd, 3rd and 4th sizes only
Dec 1 st at end of next and 0 [1,2] following 4th rows.
Work 1 row.

All sizes
Cast off 34 sts at beg of next row. *57 sts.*
Work 1 row.
Next row – Cast off 6, K to last 2 sts, K 2 tog.
Next row – K.
Next row – Cast off 6, K to end.
Next row – K.
Rep last 4 rows again.
Now cast off 6 sts at beg of next and following alt row.
Work 1 row.
Cast off remaining 19 sts.
With right side facing and A, knit up 43 [46,49,52] sts along lower edge. Cast off knitwise.

LEFT FRONT
With A, cast on 116 [119,121,123] sts and work 19 [22,24,27] rows in stripe patt.

Shape neck as follows:
Inc 1 st at beg (end,end,beg) of next and 3 following 4th rows, then at the same edge on following 3rd row. Work 1 row.
Cast on 13 sts at end [beg,beg,end] of next row. *134 [137,139,141] sts.*
Work 13 rows.
Dec 1 st at end [beg,beg,end] of next row and at same edge on 2 following 14th rows. *131 [134,136,138] sts.*
Work 11 [12,14,15] rows.

Shape armhole by casting off 36 [38,40,41] sts at end of next row. Break yarn.
Rejoin yarn to remaining sts, and dec 1 st at beg of next and following 3 [3,2,2] alt rows.
Work 1 [3,3,3] rows.

2nd, 3rd and 4th sizes only
Dec 1 st at beg of next and 0 [1,2] following 4th rows.
Work 1 row.

All sizes
Cast off 34 sts at end of next row. *57 sts.*
Break yarn.
Rejoin yarn to remaining sts and work as follows:
Next row – Cast off 6, K to end.
Next row – K2 tog, K to end.
Next row – Cast off 6, K to end.
Next row – K.
Rep last 4 rows again.
Now cast off 6 sts at beg of next and following alt row.
Cast off remaining 19 sts.
With right side facing and A, knit up 43 [46,49,52] sts along lower edge. Cast off knitwise.

SLEEVES – FIRST HALF (make 2)
With A, cast on 26 [27,29,30] sts and work 28 rows in stripe patt.

Shape side by inc 1 st at end of next and 7 following 10th rows. *34 [35,37,38] sts.*
Work straight until side edge measures 20 cm, ending with wrong side facing for next row.

Shape top by casting off 3 sts at beg of next row, then dec 1 st at end of next and 9 [10,9,10] following 6th rows.
Work 3 rows. Now dec 1 st at end of next and 2 [2,5,5] following 4th rows. Work 3 rows.
Cast off remaining 18 sts.

SLEEVES – SECOND HALF (make 2)
With A, cast on 76 [78,81,83] sts and work 42 rows in stripe patt.
Now dec 1 st at end of next row, and at the same edge on following 17 [19,23,27] rows. *58 [58,57,55] sts.*
Next row – Cast off 12, K to last 2 sts, K2 tog.
Next row – K2 tog, K to end.
Next row – Cast off 3 sts, K to last 2 sts, K2 tog.
Rep last 2 rows 2 [2,3,3] more times. *30 [30,24,22] sts.*

1st and 2nd sizes only

Next row – K2 tog, K to end.

Next row – Cast off 3, K to last 3 sts, K3 tog.

All sizes

Next row – K2 tog, K to end.

Next row – Cast off 4 sts, K to last 3 [3,3,0] sts, K3 tog 1 [1,1,0] times. *17 sts.*

Next row – K.

Next row – Cast off 4 sts, K to end.

Rep last 2 rows twice more.

Cast off remaining 5 sts.

With right side facing and A, knit up 26 [27,29,30] sts along lower edge.

Cast off knitwise.

COLLAR (make 2)

With A, cast on 44 [46,48,50] sts and work 34 rows in stripe patt.

Cast off.

With right side facing and A, knit up 14 sts along each side edge.

Cast off knitwise.

POCKET

With A, cast on 19 sts and work 28 rows in stripe patt.

Now dec 1 st at each end of next and 2 following alt rows. *13 sts.*

Cast off.

TO MAKE UP

Do not press.

Neatly join centre-front seam. Join centre-back seam to button border extension. Place right border extension over left, and catch bases neatly in position.

Neatly join centre-sleeve seams, placing first and second halves together.

Join shoulder, side and sleeve seams; insert sleeves as in photograph, gathering extra fullness across top.

Sew cast-off edges of collar pieces to neck edges, placing collar edges to centre-front seam and centre back, leaving border extensions free.

Sew buttons on left back to correspond with buttonholes. Sew pocket neatly in position as in photograph.

N°. 2607
GIRL'S JUMPER
PATONS SUPER CRÊPE, 3-PLY WEIGHT (or PATONS SUPER, or BEEHIVE, SCOTCH FINGERING WOOL, 3-PLY)

PRICE 2ᴰ·
This price only applies in Great Britain and Northern Ireland

PATONS & BALDWINS

A "P&B" PUBLICATION

Ronald and Rona

His and Hers – Sleeveless Cardigan (1938)

Originally designed for formal occasions – men only – we have created a feminine version as well (same pattern, lots of sizes). This versatile waistcoat, which is simple and quick to knit, goes with a variety of casual or more formal outfits. You'll be tempted to make it in several colours. Suitable for beginners.

To fit bust/chest		cm	86	91	97	102	107	112
	(approx)	in	34	36	38	40	42	44
Length from top of shoulders		cm	47	48	49	51	52	53
	(approx)	in	$18\frac{1}{2}$	19	$19\frac{1}{2}$	20	$20\frac{1}{2}$	21
Patons Clansman DK		50 g balls	6	7	7	7	8	8

Pair each Nos. $3\frac{1}{4}$ mm and 4 mm needles.
4 buttons.

Tension
On No. 4 mm needles, 22 sts and 30 rows to 10 cm (stocking stitch).

Abbreviations
K = knit; P = purl; st = stitch; inc = increase; dec = decrease; beg = beginning; alt = alternate; tog = together; cm = centimetres; mm = millimetres; in = inches.

LEFT FRONT
With No. $3\frac{1}{4}$ mm needles, cast on 62 [66,70,80,84,88] sts and work 4 rows in K1, P1 rib for man's version and 24 [24,24,28,28,28] rows for woman's version.

Man's version only
Work 1st buttonhole as follows:
Next 2 rows – Rib 17 [19,21,23,25,27], cast off 2 sts, rib to end and back, casting on 2 sts over cast-off sts.
Work 12 [12,12,16,16,16] rows in rib.
Next 2 rows – Work 2nd buttonhole as 1st.
Work 4 rows in rib.

** *Both versions – 1st, 2nd and 3rd sizes only*
Change to No. 4 mm needles. Starting with a K row and working in stocking stitch, *dec* 1 st at *end* of 1st row *and at same edge* on 19 following 3rd rows, *at the same time inc* 1 st at *beg* of 9th and 5 following 8th rows. *48 [52,56] sts.*

4th, 5th and 6th sizes
Change to No. 4 mm needles. Starting with a K row and working in stocking stitch, dec 1 st at *end* of next and 12 [15,18] following alt rows, *at the same time inc* 1 st at *beg* of 9th and following 16th row. *69 [70, 71] sts.*
Work 1 [2,2] rows.
Now dec 1 st at *front edge* on next and 8 [6,4] following 3rd rows, *at the same time* inc 1 st at *beg* of 16th row from previous inc. *60 [64,67] sts.*

All sizes
Work 2 [2,0,2,2,2] rows.

Continue shaping front edge and **shape armhole** as follows:
Next row – Cast off 3 [3,3,4,4,4] sts, K to last 2 [2,0,2,2,2] sts, K2 tog 1 [1,0,1,1,1] time.
Work 1 row.
Dec 1 st at *armhole edge* on next 7 [7,9,9,9,9] rows, then following 3 [4,3,2,3,4] alt rows, *at the same time dec* 1 st at *front edge* on 5 [5,6,5,5,6] following 3rd rows. *29 [32,35,40,42,43] sts.*
Keeping armhole edge straight continue dec at *front edge* on 4 [13,15,18,19,19] following 3rd rows. *25 [19,20,22,23,24] sts.*

1st size only
Now dec at *front edge* on 7 following 4th rows. *18 sts.*

All sizes
Work 2 [5,3,2,3,2] rows, ending with a P row.
Cast off 6 [7,6,8,7,8] sts at beg of next row, then 6 [6,7,7,8,8] sts at beg of 2 following alt rows.

MAN'S PULL-OVER
FROM PATON'S SUPER OR BEEHIVE FINGERING

RIGHT FRONT

With No. 3¼ mm needles, cast on 62 [66,70,80,84,88] sts and work 4 rows in K1, P1 rib for woman's version and 24 [24,24,28,28,28] rows for man's version.

Woman's version only
Work 1st buttonhole as follows:
Next 2 rows – Rib 43 [45,47,55,56,59], cast off 2 sts, rib to end and back, casting on 2 sts above cast-off stitches. Work 12 [12,12,16,16,16] rows in rib.
Next 2 rows – Work 2nd buttonhole as 1st.
Work 4 rows rib.
Complete to match Left Front from ** to end, reversing all shapings.

BACK

With No. 3¼ mm needles, cast on 82 [88,94,106,112,118] sts and work in K1, P1 rib for 24 [24,24,28,28,28] rows.

Change to No. 4 mm needles. Starting with a K row, work in stocking stitch, **shaping sides** by inc 1 st at each end of 9th and every following 8th [8th,8th,16th,16th,16th] row, until there are 94 [100,106,112,118,124] sts.
Work 9 [9,7,11,11,11] rows.

Shape armholes by casting off 3 [3,3,4,4,4] sts at beg of next 2 rows, then dec 1 st at each end of next 7 [7,9,9,9,9] rows.
Work 1 row.
Now dec 1 st at each end of the next and following 2 [3,2,1,2,3] alt rows.
Work 43 [43,49,57,59,59] rows, ending with a P row.

Shape shoulders by casting off 6 [7,6,8,7,8] sts at beg of next 2 rows, then 6 [6,7,7,8,8] sts at beg of following 4 rows.
Cast off remaining 32 [34,36,38,40,42] sts.

TO MAKE UP

Omitting ribbing, press parts lightly on wrong side, following instructions on yarn band.
Join shoulder and side seams.

Armhole borders
With No. 3¼ mm needles, cast on 5 sts and work in rib as follows:
1st row (right side) – K2, P1, K2.
2nd row – K1 (P1, K1) twice.
Rep last 2 rows until border fits all round armhole. Starting at side seam, sew border in position stretching it slightly to fit shaped curves.
Cast off. Join border edges.

Left front border – man's version
With No. 3¼ mm needles, cast on 7 sts and work in rib as follows:
1st row (right side) – K2, P1, K1, P1, K2.
2nd row – K1 (P1, K1) 3 times.
Rep last 2 rows once.
Next 2 rows – **make 1st buttonhole:** rib 2, cast off 2, rib to end and back, casting on 2 sts above cast-off stitches.
Work in rib until border is level with 2nd buttonhole on Left Front, ending with a 2nd row.
Next 2 rows – Make 2nd buttonhole as 1st.
Now continue in rib until border, when slightly stretched, fits up Left Front and round to centre back of neck, sewing in position as you go.
Cast off.

Right front border – man's version
Work as for left border, omitting buttonholes.

Left front border – woman's version
As man's right border.

Right front border – woman's version
As man's left border.
Join borders at centre back.
Press seams.
Sew on buttons to correspond with buttonholes.

Herbert

Man's Sleeveless Slipover (1940s)

This colourful pullover strikes a cheerful note; it is quick to make in two shades of double knitting.

To fit chest						
	cm	91	97	102	107
(approx)	in	36	38	40	42

Length from top of shoulders					
	cm	51	52	53	54
(approx)	in	20	20½	21	21½

Patons Beehive DK					
Main shade (A)	50 g balls	4	4	4	5
Contrast shade (B)	50 g balls	2	2	2	2

Pair each Nos. 3¼ mm and 4 mm needles.

Tension
On No. 4 mm needles, 22 sts and 30 rows to 10 cm (stocking st).

Abbreviations
K = knit; P = purl; st = stitch; dec = decrease; M1 = make a stitch by picking up horizontal loop lying before next stitch and working into the back of it; tog = together; patt = pattern; rep = repeat; beg = beginning; alt = alternate; cm = centimetres; mm = millimetres; in = inches; A = main shade; B = contrast.

Note
When working colour patt, divide yarns into separate balls for each section so that yarns are not carried across back of work. Twist yarns on wrong side when changing colour to avoid making a hole.

BACK
With No. 3¼ mm needles and B, cast on 88 [94,100,104] sts and work in K1, P1 rib for 8 cm.
Next row – Rib 2 [5,2,4] (M1, rib 7 [7,8,8]) 12 times, M1, rib 2 [5,2,4]. *101 [107,113,117] sts.*

Change to No. 4 mm needles. Joining in separate balls of colour as required, work colour patt as follows:
1st row (right side) – K10 [13,11,13] B, (1A, 15 [15,17,17] B) 5 times, 1A, 10 [13,11,13] B
2nd row – P as 1st row.
3rd row – As 1st row.

4th row – P9 [12,10,12] B (3A, 13 [13,15,15] B) 5 times, 3A, 9 [12,10,12] B.
5th row – K as 4th row.
6th row – As 4th row.
7th row – K8 [11,9,11] B, (5A, 11 [11,13,13] B) 5 times, 5A, 8 [11,9,11] B.
8th row – P as 7th row.
9th row – As 7th row.
10th row – P0 [1,0,0] A, 7 [9,8,10] B, (7A, 9 [9,11,11] B) 5 times, 7A, 7 [9,8,10] B, 0 [1,0,0] A.
11th row – K as 10th row.
12th row – As 10th.
13th row – K0 [2,0,0] A, 6 [7,7,9] B, (9A, 7 [7,9,9] B) 5 times, 9A, 6 [7,7,9] B, 0 [2,0,0] A.
14th row – P as 13th row.
15th row – As 13th row.
16th row – P0 [3,0,1] A, 5 [5,6,7] B, (11A, 5 [5,7,7] B) 5 times, 11A, 5 [5,6,7] B, 0 [3,0,1] A.
17th row – K as 16th row.
18th row – As 16th.
19th row – K1 [4,0,2] A, 3 [3,5,5] B, (13A, 3 [3,5,5] B) 6 times, 1 [4,0,2] A.
20th row – P as 19th row.
21st row – As 19th.
22nd row – P2 [5,1,3]A, 1[1,3,3] B, (15A, 1 [1,3,3] B) 6 times, 2 [5,1,3] A.
23rd row – K as 22nd row.
24th row – As 22nd row.

3rd and 4th sizes only
25th row – K2 [4] A, 1B, (17A, 1B) 6 times, 2 [4] A.
26th row – P as 25th row.
27th row – As 25th row.
28th row – P, A.

All sizes

Break B and continue in A as follows:

1st row – K2 [5,2,4], (P1, K15 [15,17,17]) 6 times, P1, K2 [5,2,4].

2nd row – P.

Rep last 2 rows until Back measures 28 cm, ending with a 2nd row.

Keeping patt correct, **shape armholes** by casting off 4 sts at beg of next 2 rows, then dec 1 st at each end of next 5 [7,9,9] rows. Work 1 row. Now dec 1 st at each end of next and following 3 [2,2,2] alt rows. *75 [79,81,85] sts.* **

Continue straight in patt until Back measures 51 [52,53,54] cm ending with a 2nd row.

Shape shoulders by casting off 6 [7,8,7] sts at beg of next 2 rows, then 7 [7,7,8] sts at beg of following 4 rows.

Leave remaining 35 [37,37,39] sts on a length of yarn.

FRONT

Work as for Back to **.

Continue straight in patt until Front measures 42 [43,44,45] cm, ending with a 2nd row.

Divide for neck as follows:

Next row – Patt 28 [29,30,31], K2 tog, turn and leave remaining sts on a spare needle.

First side

Continue on these 29 [30,31,32] sts for first side and dec 1 st at neck edge on next 6 rows. Work 1 row. Now dec 1 st at neck edge on next and following 2 alt rows. *20 [21,22,23] sts.*

Work straight until Front matches Back at armhole edge, ending with a 2nd row.

Shape shoulder by casting off 6 [7,8,7] sts at beg of next row, then 7 [7,7,8] sts at beg of 2 following alt rows.

Second side

With right side facing, leave centre 15 [17,17,19] sts on length of yarn, rejoin yarn to remaining sts, K2 tog, patt to end. Finish to match first side, reversing shapings.

TO MAKE UP

Do not press.

Join right shoulder seam.

Neckband

With right side facing, No. 3¼ mm needles and A, start at left front shoulder and knit up 26 sts down left side of neck, K15 [17,17,19] sts from centre, knit up 26 sts up right side, then K35 [37,37,39] sts from back neck. *102 [106,106,110] sts.*

Work 6 rows in K1, P1 rib. Cast off evenly in rib.

Join left shoulder seam and neckband.

Armbands

With right side facing, No. 3¼ mm needles and A, knit up 112 [118,124,130] sts all round each armhole.

Work 6 rows in K1, P1 rib. Cast off evenly in rib.

Join side seams and armbands.

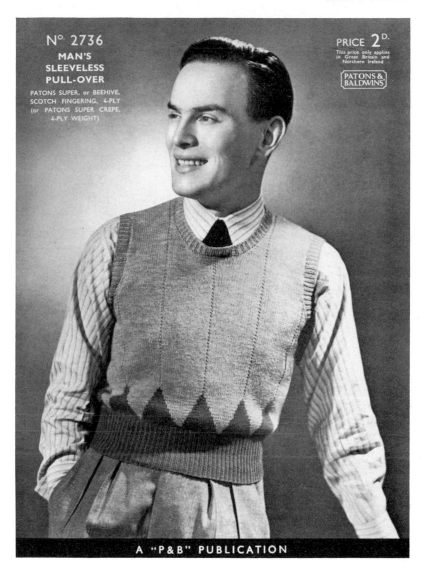

N° 2736
MAN'S
SLEEVELESS
PULL-OVER

PATONS SUPER, or BEEHIVE,
SCOTCH FINGERING, 4-PLY
(or PATONS SUPER CREPE,
4-PLY WEIGHT)

PRICE 2 D.
This price only applies
in Great Britain and
Northern Ireland

PATONS &
BALDWINS

A "P&B" PUBLICATION

Bunch of Grapes

Woman's Sweater and Cardigan (1941)

Ann Sheridan would have loved this forties twin set. Alas. the bobbly grape pattern is definitely not for beginners. You could knit the two garments in the same colour or in closely harmonizing colours.

To fit bust		cm	81	86	91	97
	(approx)	in	32	34	36	38
Sweater Approximate length from top of shoulders		cm	53	54	55	56
		in	21	21½	22	22½
Approximate sleeve seam		cm	10	10	10	10
		in	4	4	4	4
Patons Clansman 4 ply	50 g balls		8	8	9	9
Cardigan Approximate length from top of shoulders		cm	55	56	57	58
		in	21½	22	22½	23
Approximate sleeve seam		cm	45	45	45	45
		in	17½	17½	17½	17½
Patons Clansman 4 ply	50 g balls		10	11	11	12

Pair each Nos. 2¾ mm and 3¼ mm needles.
6 buttons for cardigan.

Tension
Pattern is based on tension of 28 sts and 36 rows to
10 cm on No. 3¼ mm needles (stocking st).

Abbreviations
K = knit; P = purl; st = stitch; tog = together; tbl
= through back of loops; dec = decrease; inc =
increase; patt = pattern; rep = repeat; beg =
beginning; alt = alternate; MB = make bobble as
follows: (K1, yarn forward, K1, yarn forward, K1)
all in next st, turn, K5, turn, K5, slip the 4th, 3rd,
2nd and 1st of these sts over the 5th – this
completes bobble; cm = centimetres; in = inches;
mm = millimetres.

Note
Where a number of stitches is given, this refers to
the basic number and does not include those made
in bobble.

SWEATER

BACK AND FRONT ALIKE
With No. 2¾ mm needles, cast on 103
[111,117,125] sts and work in rib as follows.
1st row (right side) – K1, *P1, K1; rep from * to
end.
2nd row – P1, *K1, P1; rep from * to end. Rep last
2 rows until work measures 10 cm, ending with a
2nd row, inc 10 sts evenly on last row. *113
[121,127,135] sts.*

Change to No. 3¼ mm needles and work in patt as
follows:
1st row (right side) – P1 [5,4,2], (K1, P4) 1 [1,2,3]
times, *MB, (P4, K1) 3 times, P4; rep from * to last 7
[11,14,18] sts, MB, (P4, K1) 1 [1,2,3] times, P1
[5,4,2].
2nd row – K1 [5,4,2], (P1, K4) 1 [1,2,3] times, *P1
tbl, (K4, P1) 3 times, K4; rep from * to last 7
[11,14,18] sts, P1 tbl (K4, P1) 1 [1,2,3] times, K1
[5,4,2].
3rd row – P1 [5,4,2], (K1, P4) 0 [0,1,2] times, *K1,
P3, MB, P1, MB, P3, (K1, P4) twice; rep from * to
last 12 [16,19,23] sts K1, P3, MB, P1, MB, P3, K1,
(P4, K1) 0 [0,1,2] times, P1 [5,4,2].
4th row – K1 [5,4,2], (P1, K4) 0 [0,1,2] times, *P1,
K3, P1 tbl, K1, P1 tbl, K3, (P1, K4) twice; rep from
* to last 12 [16, 19, 23] sts, P1, K3, P1 tbl, K1, P1
tbl, K3, P1, (K4, P1) 0 [0,1,2] times, K1 [5,4,2].

5th row – P1 [5,4,2], (K1, P4) 0 [0,1,2] times, *K1,
P2, (MB, P1) 3 times, P1, (K1, P4) twice; rep from *
to last 12 [16, 19, 23] sts, K1, P2, (MB, P1) 3
times, P1, K1, (P4, K1) 0 [0,1,2] times, P1 [5,4,2].
6th row – K1 [5,4,2], (P1, K4) 0 [0,1,2] times, *P1,
K2, (P1 tbl, K1) 3 times, K1, (P1, K4) twice; rep
from * to last 12 [16,19,23] sts, P1, K2, (P1 tbl,
K1) 3 times, K1, P1, (K4, P1) 0 [0,1,2] times, K1
[5,4,2].
7th row – P1 [5,3,2], (K1, P4) 3 [3,0,1] times, *MB,
(P4, K1) 3 times, P4; rep. from * to last 17 [21,4,8]
sts, MB, (P4, K1) 3 [3,0,1] times, P1 [5,3,2].
8th row – K1 [5,3,2], (P1, K4) 3 [3,0,1] times, *P1
tbl, (K4, P1) 3 times, K4; rep from * to last 17
[21,4,8] sts, P1 tbl, (K4, P1) 3 [3,0,1] times, K1
[5,3,2].
9th row – P1 [5,0,2], (K1, P4) 2 [2,0,0] times, K1
[1,0,1], P3 [3,2,3], * MB, P1, MB, P3, (K1, P4)
twice, K1, P3; rep from * to last 18 [22,5,9] sts, MB,
P1, MB, P3 [3,2,3], K1 [1,0,1], (P4, K1) 2 [2,0,0]
times, P1 [5,0,2].
10th row – K1 [5,0,2], (P1, K4) 2 [2,0,0] times, P1
[1,0,1], K3 [3,2,3], *P1 tbl, K1, P1 tbl, K3, (P1, K4)
twice, P1, K3; rep from * to last 18 [22,5,9] sts, P1
tbl, K1, P1 tbl, K3 [3,2,3], P1 [1,0,1], (K4, P1) 2
[2,0,0] times, K1 [5,0,2].
11th row – P1 [5,0,2], (K1, P4) 2 [2,0,0] times, K1
[1,0,1], P2 [2,1,2], * (MB, P1) twice, MB, P2, (K1,
P4) twice, K1, P2; rep from * to last 19 [23,6,10]
sts, (MB, P1) twice, MB, P2 [2,1,2], K1 [1,0,1], (P4,
K1) 2 [2,0,0] times, P1 (5,0,2).
12th row – K1 [5,0,2], (P1, K4) 2 [2,0,0] times, P1
[1,0,1], K2 [2,1,2], * (P1 tbl, K1) twice, P1 tbl, K2,
(P1, K4) twice, P1, K2; rep from * to last 19
[23,6,10] sts, (P1 tbl, K1) twice, P1 tbl, K2 [2,1,2],
P1 [1,0,1], (K4, P1) 2 [2,0,0] times, K1 [5,0,2].
These 12 rows form patt.**
Continue in patt until work measures approx 35 cm,
ending with 6th or 12th row of patt.

Keeping patt correct, **shape armholes** by casting off
4 sts at beg of next 2 rows, then dec 1 st at each
end of next 5 rows.
Work 1 row.
Now dec 1 st at each end of next and following 2
[4,4,6] alt rows. *89 [93,99,103] sts.*
Continue straight until armhole measures 8
[9,10,11] cm, ending with right side facing for next
row.

Keep patt correct, **divide for neck** as follows:
Next row – Patt 27 [28,29,30], work 2 tog, turn
and leave remaining sts on a spare needle.

Continue on these 28 [29,30,31] sts for first side and dec 1 st at neck edge on next 6 rows.
Work 1 row.
Now dec 1 st at neck edge on next and following 2 alt rows. *19 [20,21,22] sts.*
Continue straight until armhole measures 18 [19,20,21] cm, ending with right side facing for next row.

Shape shoulder by casting off 7 [6,7,8] sts at beg of next row, then 6 [7,7,7] sts at beg of following 2 alt rows.
With right side facing leave centre 31 [33,37,39] sts on a length of yarn, rejoin yarn to remaining sts and finish to match first side, reversing shapings.

YOKE (Back and Front alike)
With right side of work facing and No. 2¾ mm needles, knit up 34 sts down side of neck, K31 [33,37,39] sts from centre, inc 4 [2,2,4] sts evenly across centre, and knit up 34 sts up side of neck. *103 [103,107,111] sts.*
1st row – K3, *P1, K3; rep from * to end.
2nd row – P3, *K1, P3; rep from * to end.
Rep last 2 rows 4 times more.
11th row – K1, K2 tog, *P1, K1, K2 tog; rep from * to end. *77 [77,80,83] sts.*
12th row – P2, *K1, P2; rep from * to end.
13th row – K2, *P1, K2; rep from * to end.
Rep last 2 rows twice, then 12th again.
19th row – K2 tog, *P1, K2 tog; rep from * to end. *51 [51,53,55] sts.*
20th row – P1, *K1, P1; rep from * to end.
21st row – K1, *P1, K1; rep from * to end.
Rep last 2 rows once more.
Cast off loosely in rib.

SLEEVES
With No. 2¾ mm needles, cast on 71 [75, 77, 81] sts and work in K1, P1 rib as for Back and Front for 4 cm, ending with a 2nd row, and inc 10 [12,10,12] sts evenly on last row. *81 [87,87,93] sts.*

Change to No. 3¼ mm needles and work in patt as for 2nd [3rd, 3rd, 1st] sizes on Back and Front, until sleeve measures approx 10 cm, ending with 6th or 12th row of patt.

Keeping patt correct, **shape top** by casting off 4 sts at beg of next 2 rows, then dec 1 st at each end of following row.

Work 1 [1,3,3] rows.
Dec 1 st at each end of next and every alt row until 29 [33,29,29] sts remain.

2nd size only
Dec 1 st at each end of next 2 rows. *29 sts.*

All sizes
Cast off.

TO MAKE UP
Omitting ribbing, press parts lightly on wrong side following the instructions on the yarn label and taking care not to flatten the bobbles.
Join shoulder, side and sleeve seams; insert sleeves. Press seams.

CARDIGAN

BACK
Work as for Back of sweater to **.
Continue in patt until Back measures approx 36 cm, ending with 6th or 12th row of patt.

Keep patt correct, **shape armholes** by casting off 4 sts at beg of next 2 rows, then dec 1 st at each end of following 5 rows.
Work 1 row.
Now dec 1 st at each end of next and following 1 [3,3,5] alt rows. *91 [95,101,105] sts.*
Continue straight until armhole measures 19 [20,21,22] cm, ending with right side facing for next row.

Shape shoulders by casting off 8 [9,10,10] sts at beg of next 2 rows, then 9 [9,9,10] sts at beg of following 4 rows.
Cast off remaining 39 [41, 43, 45] sts.

LEFT FRONT
With No. 2¾ mm needles, cast on 51 [55,57,61] sts and work in rib as for Back, inc 5 [5,6,6] sts evenly on last row. *56 [60,63,67] sts.*

Change to 3¼ mm needles and work in patt as follows:
1st row (right side) – P1 [5,4,2], (K1, P4) 1 [1,2,3] times, * MB, (P4, K1) 3 times, P4; rep from * to last 10 sts, MB, P4, K1, P4.
2nd row – K4, P1, K4, P1 tbl, *(K4, P1) 3 times, K4, P1 tbl; rep from * to last 6 [10,13,17] sts, (K4, P1) 1 [1,2,3] times, K1 [5,4,2].
3rd row – P1 [5,4,2], (K1, P4) 0 [0,1,2] times, *K1,

P3, MB, P1, MB, P3, (K1, P4) twice; rep from * to last 15 sts, K1, P3, MB, P1, MB, P3, K1, P4.
4th row – K4, P1, K3, P1 tbl, K1, P1 tbl, K3, P1, *(K4, P1) twice, K3, P1 tbl, K1, P1 tbl, K3, P1; rep from * to last 1 [5,9,12] sts, (K4, P1) 0 [0,1,2] times, K1 [5,4,2].
5th row – P1 [5,4,2], (K1, P4) 0 [0,1,2] times, *K1, P2, (MB, P1) 3 times, P1, (K1, P4) twice; rep from * to last 15 sts, K1, P2, (MB, P1) 3 times, P1, K1, P4.
6th row – K4, P1, K1, (K1, P1 tbl) 3 times, K2, P1 (K4, P1) twice, K1, (K1, P1 tbl) 3 times, K2, P1; rep from * to last 1 [5,9,12] sts, (K4, P1) 0 [0,1,2] times, K1 [5,4,2].
7th row – P1 [5,3,2], (K1, P4) 3 [3,0,1] times, *MB, (P4, K1) 3 times, P4; rep from * to end.
8th row – *K4, (P1, K4) 3 times, P1 tbl; rep from * to last 16 [20,3,7] sts, (K4, P1) 3 [3,0,1] times, K1 [5,3,2].
9th row – P1 [5,0,2], (K1, P4) 2 [2,0,0] times, K1 [1,0,1], P3 [3,2,3], *MB, P1, MB, P3, (K1, P4) twice, K1, P3; rep from * to last st, P1.
10th row – K1, *K3, P1, (K4, P1) twice, K3, P1 tbl, K1, P1 tbl; rep from * to last 15 [19,2,6] sts, K3 [3,2,3], P1 [1,0,1], (K4, P1) 2 [2,0,0] times, K1 [5,3,2].
11th row – P1 [5,0,2], (K1, P4) 2 [2,0,0] times, K1 [1,0,1], P2 [2,1,2], *(MB, P1) twice, MB, P2, (K1, P4) twice, K1, P2; rep from * to last 2 sts, P2.
12th row – K2, *K2, P1, (K4, P1) twice, K2, P1 tbl, (K1, P1 tbl) twice; rep from * to last 14 [18,1,5] sts, K2 [2,1,2], P1 [1,0,1], (K4, P1) 2 [2,0,0] times, K1 [5,0,2].
These 12 rows form patt.
Continue in patt until Back measures approx 36 cm, ending with 6th or 12th row of patt.

Keeping patt correct, **shape armhole and front edge** as follows:
1st row – Cast off 4 sts, patt to last 2 sts, work 2 tog.
2nd row – In patt.
3rd row – Work 2 tog, patt to last 2 sts, work 2 tog.
4th row – Patt to last 2 sts, work 2 tog.
Rep 3rd and 4th rows once more, then 3rd row again.
8th row – In patt.
9th row – Work 2 tog, patt to last 2 sts, work 2 tog.
Rep 8th and 9th rows 1 [3,3,3] times more, *38 [39,42,46] sts.*

4th size only
Next row – In patt.
Next row – Work 2 tog, patt to end.
Next row – In patt.
Next row – As 9th. *43 sts.*

All sizes
Keeping armhole edge straight, continue dec at front edge on every 4th row from previous dec until 26 [27,29,30] sts remain.
Work straight until Front matches Back at armhole edge, ending with right side facing for next row.

Shape shoulder by casting off 8 [9,10,10] sts at beg of next row, then 9 [9,9,10] sts at beg of following 2 alt rows.

RIGHT FRONT
Work as for Left Front, *reversing shapings* and *reversing patt*, noting that the patt will be set as follows:
1st row (right side) – P4, K1, P4, MB, *P4, (K1, P4) 3 times, MB; rep from * to last 6 [10,13,17] sts, (P4, K1) 1 [1,2,3] times, P1 [5,4,2].
2nd row – K1 [5,4,2], (P1, K4) 1 [1,2,3] times, P1 tbl, (K4, P1) 3 times, K4; rep from * to last 10 sts, P1 tbl, K4, P1, K4.

SLEEVES
With No. 2¾ mm needles, cast on 53 [55,55,57] sts and work in rib as for Back for 7 cm, ending with a 2nd row; inc 14 [18,18,18] sts evenly on last row. *67 [73,73,75] sts.*

Change to No. 3¼ mm needles. Work in patt as for 3rd [1st,1st,4th] sizes, and shape sides by inc 1 st at each end of 13th and every following 12th row until there are 87 [93,93,95] sts, and taking inc sts into patt when appropriate. Work straight until sleeve seam measures approx 45 cm, ending with a 6th or 12th row of patt.

Keeping patt correct, **shape top** by casting off 4 sts at beg of next 2 rows, then dec 1 st at each end of following row.
Work 1 [1,1,3] rows.
Now dec 1 st at each end of next and every alt row until 33 [37,29,29] sts remain.

1st and 2nd sizes only
Dec 1 st at each end of next 2 [4] rows, *29 sts.*

All sizes
Cast off.

Bunch of Grapes (FACING PAGE TOP)

Two Turbans (FACING PAGE BOTTOM)

Herbert

TO MAKE UP

Press as for Sweater. Join shoulder, side and sleeve seams; insert sleeves.

Left front border

With No. 2¾ mm needles, cast on 9 sts and work in rib as follows:

1st row (right side) – K2, (P1, K1) 3 times, K1.

2nd row – K1, (P1, K1) 4 times.

Rep last 2 rows until border, when slightly stretched, fits up left front edge and round to centre back, sewing in position as you go along. Cast off.

Right front border

Work as for left border with the addition of 6 buttonholes, the first to come 1 cm from lower edge, the sixth level with start of front edge shaping, the remainder spaced evenly between.

First mark position of buttons on left front border, then work holes to correspond.

To make a buttonhole – 1st row (right side) – Rib 4, cast off 2, rib to end.

2nd row – Rib 3, cast on 2, rib 4.

Join borders at centre back. Press seams.

Sew on buttons.

Barbara

Woman's Jumper (1941)

Pleated and puffed shoulders, and the contrasting detail on collar, cuffs and welt, put this easy-to-knit short-sleeved jumper from the early forties in the frontline of today's fashion.

		81	86	91	97	102
To fit bust	cm	81	86	91	97	102
(approx)	in	32	34	36	38	40
Length from top of shoulders	cm	50	51	53	54	55
(approx)	in	20	20½	21	21½	22
Sleeve seam	cm	14	14	14	14	14
	in	5½	5½	5½	5½	5½
Patons Clansman 4 ply						
Main shade (B)	50 g balls	5	5	6	6	7
Contrast shade (A)	50 g balls	1	1	1	1	1

Pair each Nos. 3 mm and 3¼ mm needles.
Clasps for front opening.

Tension
On No. 3¼ mm needles, 28 sts and 36 rows to 10 cm (stocking stitch).

Abbreviations
K = knit; P = purl; st = stitch; tog = together; tbl = through back of loop; inc = increase; dec = decrease; beg = beginning; alt = alternate; rep = repeat; patt = pattern; cm = centimetres; in = inches; mm = millimetres; M1 = make a stitch by picking up horizontal loop lying before next stitch and working into back of it; B = main shade; A = contrast shade.

Note
When working colour patt, strand yarn not in use loosely across wrong side of work over not more than 3 sts at a time to keep fabric elastic. When working from chart read odd rows K from right to left and even rows P from left to right.

BACK
** With No. 3 mm needles and A, cast on 91 [99,107,115,123] sts and work 8 rows in garter stitch (every row K).
Next row – K8 [10,9,10,12], *M1, K15 [16,18,19,20]; rep from * to last 8 [9,8,10,11] sts, M1, K to end.   *97 [105,113,121,129] sts.*

Change to No. 3¼ mm needles. Join in B and work 4 rows from chart A, repeating the 8 patt sts 12 [13,14,15,16] times across and working the first st on K rows and last st on P rows as indicated. Break A.
Starting with a K row, work in stocking stitch; shape sides by inc 1 st at each end of 11th and every following 8th [8th,10th,10th,11th] row until there are 117 [125,131,139,145] sts.
Work straight until Back measures 30 [30,31,31,31] cm, ending with a P row.

Shape armholes: cast off 4 sts at beg of next 2 rows, then dec 1 st at each end of next 3 rows, then on every alt row until 91 [95,99,103,107] sts remain. Work straight until Back measures 50 [51,53,54,55] cm, ending with a P row.

Shape shoulders by casting off 8 [9,9,9,10] sts at beg of next 4 rows, then 9 [8,9,10,9] sts at beg of following 2 rows.
Cast off remaining 41 [43,45,47,49] sts.

FRONT
Work as for Back from ** until 3 rows less than Back have been worked to start of armhole shaping, ending with a K row.

Divide for front opening
Next row – P58 [62,65,69,72], cast off 1 st, P to end.
Next row – K58 [62,65,69,72], turn and leave

remaining sts on a spare needle.
Next row – K2, P to end.

Shape armhole as follows:
Next row – Cast off 4 sts, K to end.
Next row – K2, P to end.
Keeping 2 K sts at front edge, dec 1 st at armhole edge on next 3 rows, then every alt row until 45 [47,49,51,53] sts remain.
Work straight until Front measures 42 [43,45,46,47] cm, ending with a K row.

Shape neck as follows:
Next row – Cast off 7 [7,8,8,8] sts, P to end.
Dec 1 st at neck edge on every row until 25 [26,27,28,29] sts remain.
Work straight until Front measures same as Back to shoulders, ending with a P row.

Shape shoulder by casting off 8 [9,9,9,10] sts at beg of next and following alt row. Work 1 row. Cast off remaining 9 [8,9,10,9] sts.

With right side facing, rejoin yarn to remaining sts, K to end.
Next row – P to last 2 sts, K2.
Complete to match first side, reversing shapings.

SLEEVES
With No. 3 mm needles and A, cast on 56 [58,60,62,62] sts and work 8 rows in garter stitch.
Next row – K4 [5,2,3,3], *M1, K6 [6,7,7,7], rep from * to last 4 [5,2,3,3] sts, M1, K to end.   65 [67,69,73,73] sts.

Change to No. 3¼ mm needles. Join in B and work 4 rows from chart B, repeating the 8 patt sts 8 [8,8,9,9] times across, working the first 1 [2,3,1,1] and last 0 [1,2,0,0] sts on K rows and first 0 [1,2,0,0] sts and last 1 [2,3,1,1] sts on P rows as indicated. Break A.
Starting with a K row, work in stocking stitch; inc 1 st at each end of 5th row. Work 3 rows.
Next row – K26 [27,28,30,30], inc in next st, K12, inc in next st, K27 [28,29,31,31].
Work 3 rows.
Continue inc 1 st at each side of centre 12 sts on next and every 4th row, *and at the same time* inc 1 st at each end of next and every 8th row until there are 91 [93,95,99,99] sts.
Work 1 row.

Shape top by casting off 4 sts at beg of next 2 rows.
Continue inc 1 st at each side of centre 12 sts on next and every 4th row, *at the same time* dec 1 st at each end of next and every alt row until 57 [57,59,61,61] sts remain.
Work 1 row.
Cast off.

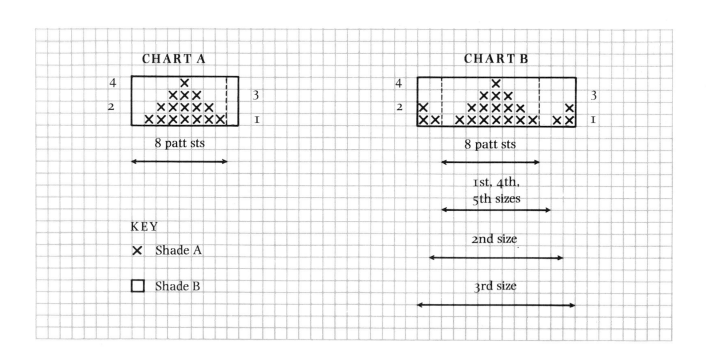

CHART A

4
2

3
1

8 patt sts

CHART B

4
2

3
1

8 patt sts

1st, 4th, 5th sizes

2nd size

3rd size

KEY

☒ Shade A

☐ Shade B

COLLAR

With No. 3¼ mm needles and A, cast on 80 [80,88,88,96] sts and work 8 rows in garter stitch.

Next row – K8 [8,8,8,10], *M1, K16 [16,18,18,19], rep from * to last 8 [8,8,8,10] sts, M1, K to end. *85 [85,93,93,101] sts.*

Join in B and work as follows:

1st row – K6 in A, *K1 in B, K7 in A, rep from * to last 7 sts, K1 in B, K6 in A.

2nd row – K6 in A, P2 in B, *P5 in A, P3 in B, rep from * to last 13 sts, P5 in A, P2 in B, K6 in A.

3rd row – K6 in A, K3 in B, * K3 in A, K5 in B, rep from * to last 12 sts, K3 in A, K3 in B, K6 in A.

4th row – K6 in A, P4 in B, *P1 in A, P7 in B, rep from * to last 11 sts, P1 in A, P4 in B, K6 in A.

5th row – K6 in A, K73 [73,81,81,89] in B, join in 2nd ball of A and K6 in A.

6th row – K6 in A, P73 [73,81,81,89] in B, K6 in A. Rep 5th and 6th rows until work measures 10 cm, ending with a 6th row. Cast off.

TO MAKE UP

Press, following instructions on the yarn labels. Join shoulder, side and sleeve seams. Make a pleat in centre at top of sleeve head, approx 5 cm wide. Insert sleeves. Sew collar in position, placing ends to edges of front opening. Sew clasps in position at even intervals at neck opening.

Two Turbans

(1942)

Straight from the war-time factory worker to today's high fashion. Version A has a crown, while version B is a simple, elegant twist that can be worn as a headband in the evening if you knit in a hint of Lurex.

TURBAN-STYLE HAT (Version A, with crown)

Materials
2 50 g balls Patons Beehive DK.
Pair No. 4 mm needles.
Small quantity of wadding.

Measurements
To fit average woman's head – width all round head-piece when slightly stretched is 56 cm.

Tension
Pattern is based on tension of 20 sts and 29 rows to 10 cm on No. 4 mm needles (stocking st).

Abbreviations
K = knit; P = purl; tbl = through back of loop; st = stitch; inc = increase; rep = repeat; alt = alternate; cm = centimetres; in = inches; mm = millimetres.

CROWN
Cast on 36 sts.
1st and 2nd rows – K all sts tbl.
3rd row – * K3, tbl, inc in next st, rep from * to last 4 sts, K4 tbl. *44 sts.*
4th row – P to last 3 sts, inc in next st, P2.
5th row – K1 tbl, inc in next st, K all remaining sts tbl.
Rep 4th and 5th rows 3 times more, then 4th row again. *53 sts **.*
Leave these sts on a spare needle.
Work another piece the same to **, but reverse shaping.
Next row – K all sts tbl to last st, inc in last st, K all sts from spare needle tbl. *107 sts.*
Next row – P.
Next row – K all sts tbl.
Rep last 2 rows until Crown measures 7 cm from this point, ending with a P row.
Shape as follows:
1st row – (K10 tbl, K2 tog tbl) 8 times, K1 tbl

2nd and every alt row – P.
3rd row – (K9 tbl, K2 tog tbl) 8 times, K1 tbl.
5th row – (K8 tbl, K2 tog tbl) 8 times, K1 tbl.
Continue thus until 17 sts remain, ending with a P row.
Next row – (K2 tog tbl) 8 times, K1 tbl. *10 sts.*
Break yarn, thread through remaining sts, draw up and fasten off firmly.

BAND
Cast 28 sts.
1st row – K.
2nd row – K11 tbl, turn.
3rd row – K to end.
4th row – K22 tbl, turn.
5th row – K to end.
6th row – K all sts tbl.
7th row – K1, inc in next st, K to last 3 sts, K2 tog, K1.
Rep 6th and 7th rows until Band measures 26 cm at longer edge, ending with a 6th row.

Continue as follows:
1st row – K1, (K2 tog) 13 times, K1. *15 sts.*
2nd row – K all sts tbl.
3rd row – K1, inc in next st, K to last 3 sts, K2 tog, K1.
Rep 2nd and 3rd rows until Band measures 63 cm at longer edge, ending with a 2nd row.

Continue as follows:
1st row – K1, inc in each of next 13 sts, K1. *28 sts.*
2nd row – K all sts tbl.
3rd row – K1, inc in next st, K to last 3 sts, K2 tog, K1.
Rep 2nd and 3rd rows until Band measures 84 cm at longer edge, ending with a 2nd row.
Next row – K22, turn.
Next row – K all sts tbl.
Next row – K11, turn.
Next row – K all sts tbl.
Cast off.

Nº 3814
LADIES' TURBANS
CAIRN RIMPLE WOOL

PRICE 3D.
This price only applies
in Great Britain and
Northern Ireland

PATONS &
BALDWINS

TO MAKE UP
Join back seam of Crown.
Sew one edge of Band around cast-on edge of Crown,
easing it slightly to within 1 cm of the peak in front,
leaving ends free for front twist. Pad the Band at the
front from the increasings, sew to form a roll and
twist the ends to form a knot at the front as in the
picture. Secure the ends neatly.

TURBAN WITHOUT CROWN (Version B)
Work as for Band of Version A.
Pad the band at the front from the increasings.
Sew to form a roll and twist the ends to form a knot
in front as in the picture.
Secure the ends neatly.

Beryl

Woman's Sweater with Ribbed Yoke (1943)

We've adapted the Hedy Lamarr look of the original for our pretty version in soft blue, with its charming puff sleeves and demure neckline. It's simple to knit, in stocking stitch with a ribbed yoke and welt; ease the sleeves carefully in at the shoulder seam, and use a wire brush to fluff up the yarn.

To fit bust			81	86	91	97
	(approx)	cm	81	86	91	97
		in	32	34	36	38
Length from top of shoulders		cm	49	50	51	52
	(approx)	in	19	19½	20	20½
Sleeve seam		cm	10	11	11	12
	(approx)	in	4	4½	4½	5
Patons Promise		40 g balls	5	6	6	7

Pair each Nos. 3¾ mm and 5 mm needles.
Fancy button.

Tension
On No. 5 mm needles, 19 sts and 25 rows to 10 cm (stocking stitch).

Abbreviations
K = knit; P = purl; st = stitch; tog = together; inc = increase; dec = decrease; beg = beginning; alt = alternate; rep = repeat; tbl = through back of loops; sl 1 = slip 1; psso = pass slip stitch over; M1 = make a stitch by picking up horizontal loop lying before next stitch and working into back of it; cm = centimetres; in = inches; mm = millimetres.

BACK
With No. 3¾ mm needles, cast on 68 [74,78,84] sts and work in K1, P1 rib for 8 cm.

Change to No. 5 mm needles and, starting with a K row, work 2 rows stocking stitch.
Continue in stocking stitch, shaping sides by inc 1 st at each end of next and every following 8th row until there are 78 [84,88,94] sts.
Work straight until Back measures 31 cm, ending with a P row.

Shape armholes by casting off 6 sts at beg of next 2 rows, then dec 1 st at each end of next 3 [3,5,5] rows. Work 1 row. Now dec 1 st at each end of next and every alt row until 60 [64,66,70] sts remain. Work straight until armhole measures 7 [8,9,10] cm, ending with a P row and inc 11 sts evenly in this row. *71 [75,77,81] sts.*
Next row – P1, *K1, P1; rep from * to end.
Next row – K1, *P1, K1; rep from * to end.
Rep last 2 rows until armhole measures 18 [19,20,21] cm, ending with right side facing for next row.

Shape shoulders by casting off 6 [8,8,8] sts at beg of next 2 rows, then 7 [7,7,8] sts at beg of following 4 rows.**
Cast off remaining 31 [31,33,33] sts.

FRONT
Work as for Back to **, ending with right side facing for next row.
Next row – K2, *P1, K1; rep from * to last st, K1.
Next row – K1, *P1, K1; rep from * to end.
Next row – K2, *P1, K1; rep from * to last st, K1.
Next row – K1, P1, K2 tog tbl, rib to last 4 sts, K2 tog, P1, K1.
Next row – K2, P2, *K1, P1; rep from * to last 3 sts, P1, K2.
Next row – K1, P1, K2 tog tbl, rib to last 4 sts, K2 tog, P1, K1.
Rep last 4 rows until 7 sts remain. Work 1 row.
Next row – K1, P1, sl1, K2 tog, psso, P1, K1.
Next row – K1, P3 tog, K1.
Cast off.

Nº 2673
LADY'S JUMPER
FUZZY-WUZZY ANGORA

PRICE 2ᴰ·
This price only applies in Great Britain and Northern Ireland

PATONS & BALDWINS

A "P&B" PUBLICATION

SLEEVES

With No. 3¾ mm needles, cast on 48 [50,52,54] sts and work in K1, P1 rib for 7 cm.

Next row – Rib 5 [6,6,7], (M1, rib 1) 38 [38,40,40] times, rib to end. *86 [88,92,94] sts.*

Change to No. 5 mm needles. Starting with a K row, work in stocking stitch for 3 [3,4,4] cm, ending with a P row.

Shape top by casting off 3 sts at beg of next 2 rows. Then dec 1 st at each end of next and every alt row until 50 sts remain, ending with a P row.

Next 2 rows – Work to last 4 sts, turn.

Next 2 rows – Work to last 8 sts, turn.

Next 2 rows – Work to last 12 sts, turn.

Next 2 rows – Work to last 16 sts, turn.

Next 2 rows – K to last 20 sts, turn and P to end.

Next row – K2 tog 5 times, K3 tog 10 times, K2 tog 5 times. *20 sts.*

Cast off.

TO MAKE UP

Do not press.

Join shoulder, side and sleeve seams; insert sleeves. Fold front triangle over to right side of garment (triangle point at start of yoke ribbing) and secure by sewing a fancy button through triangle point and sweater.

Summertime

Woman's Striped Patterned Top (1945)

This evokes memories of Ealing comedies and the long hot months of British Double Summer Time. Our modern version will take you through the hottest weather in cool cotton yarn; it is knitted in two colours in a fairly simple lacy pattern.

			81	86	91	97	102
To fit bust		cm	81	86	91	97	102
	(approx)	in	32	34	36	38	40
Length from top of shoulders		cm	51	52	53	54	55
	(approx)	in	20	20½	21	21½	22
Patons Cotton Soft							
Main shade (A)		50 g balls	4	4	4	5	5
Contrast shade (B)		50 g balls	2	2	2	3	3

Pair each Nos. 3¼ mm and 4 mm needles.
No. 3.50 mm crochet hook.
6 buttons.

Tension
On No. 4 mm needles, 22 sts and 29 rows to 10 cm (stocking st).

Abbreviations
K = knit; P = purl; st = stitch; tog = together; inc = increase; dec = decrease; patt = pattern; rep = repeat; beg = beginning; alt = alternate; yfwd = yarn forward; yrn = yarn round needle; tbl – through back of loop; cm = centimetres; in = inches; mm = millimetres; A = main shade; B = contrast shade.

BACK
With No. 3¼ mm needles and A, cast on 72 [78,84,90,96] sts and work in K1, P1 rib for 10 cm, inc 1 st at centre of last row. *73 [79,85,91,97] sts.*

Change to No. 4 mm needles. Work in patt and shape sides as follows:
1st row (right side) – In A, K.
2nd row – In A, P.
3rd to 6th rows – Rep 1st and 2nd rows twice.
7th row – In B, K and inc 1 st at each end of row.
8th row – In B, K.
9th row – In B, P1,* yrn, P2 tog; rep from * to end.
10th row – In B, K.
11th to 18th rows – As 1st to 7th, but this time inc 1 st at each end of 14th row.
19th row – In B, P1, * yrn, P2 tog tbl; rep from * to end.

20th row – In B, K.
These 20 rows form patt.
Continue in patt and continue shaping sides by inc 1 st at each end of next and every following 7th row, until there are 89 [95,101,107,113] sts.**
Continue straight in patt until Back measures 50 [51,52,53,54] cm, ending with right side facing for next row.

Shape shoulders by casting off 8 [7,9,8,10] sts at beg of next 2 rows, then 7 [8,8,9,9] sts at beg of following 6 rows. *31 [33,35,37,39] sts.*
Break A.

Change to No. 3¼ mm needles and work picot border in B as follows:
1st row – K.
2nd row – P.
3rd row – K.
4th row – P.
5th row – K1,* yfwd, K2 tog; rep from * to end.
6th row – P.
7th row – K.
8th row – P.
Cast off.

FRONT
Work as for Back to **.
Continue straight in patt until Front measures 44 [45,46,46,47] cm, ending with right side facing for next row.

Keeping patt correct, **divide for neck** as follows:
Next row – Patt 35 [37,39,41,43], K2 tog, turn and leave remaining sts on a spare needle.
Continue on these 36 [38,40,42,44] sts for first side

and dec 1 st neck edge on next 4 rows. Work 1 row. Dec 1 st on neck edge of next and following 2 alt rows. 29 [31,33,35,37] sts. Work straight until Front measures 50 [51,52,53,54] cm, ending with right side facing for next row.

Shape shoulder by casting off 8 [7,9,8,10] sts at beg of next row, then 7 [8,8,9,9] sts at beg of following 3 alt rows.
With right side facing, leave centre 15 [17,19,21,23] sts on a length of yarn, rejoin appropriate yarn to remaining 37 [39,41,43,45] sts, K2 tog, patt to end. Complete to match first side.

Using No. 3¼ needles, work **picot border** in B as follows:
With right side facing, knit up 18 [18,18,20,20] sts down left side of neck, K15 [17,19,21,23] from centre, then knit up 18 [18,18,20,20] sts up left side. 51 [53,55,61,63] sts.
Finish picot border as for Back, from 2nd row.

TO MAKE UP
Do not press.
Join shoulder seams, leaving 10 cm free at either side of neck.
Fold picot borders along row of holes on wrong side and slip-hem into position.

Shoulder openings
With crochet hook, work 2 rows of double crochet round each opening; working 3 button loops on front edges on 2nd row – one on picot border, the remaining 2 evenly spaced. (To make a button loop – 2 chain, miss 1, double crochet.)

Armhole picot borders
Place markers on side edges of Back and Front, 18 [19,20,21,22] cm either side of shoulder seams. With right side facing, No. 3¼ mm needles and B, knit up 79 [83,87,93,97] sts between markers. Finish as for Back picot border from 2nd row.
Fold picot borders along row of holes on wrong side and slip-hem into position. Remove markers.

Join side seams.
Sew buttons to back shoulder edges to correspond with button loops.

Barbara

Beryl

Lilli

Lilli

Striped Cowl-neck Top (1951)

Remember Audrey Hepburn, Leslie Caron? Theirs was the look that was epitomized by Christian Dior: calf-length swirling skirts, tiny waists and gamine haircuts ... and isn't that a very young Jean Marsh in the original picture?

To fit bust			cm	81	86	91	97
	(approx)	in		32	34	36	38
Length from top of shoulders			cm	54	56	57	58
	(approx)	in		21½	22	22½	23
Patons Beehive Chunky							
Main shade (A)		50 g balls		5	6	6	6
Contrast shade (B)		50 g balls		4	4	5	5

Pair each Nos. 5 mm and 6 mm needles.

Tension
On No. 6 mm needles, 15 sts and 30 rows to 10 cm (garter st).

Abbreviations
K = knit; P = purl; st = stitch; inc = increase; dec = decrease; beg = beginning; alt = alternate; rep = repeat; patt = pattern; cm = centimetres; in = inches; mm = millimetres; A = main shade; B = contrast shade.

BACK
** Using No. 5 mm needles and A, cast on 65 [69,73,77] sts and K 5 rows (1st row is wrong side). Change to No. 6 mm needles, join in B and work in garter st (every row K) stripes of 2 rows B, 2 rows A. Dec 1 st at each end of 5th and every following 6th row until 57 [61,65,69] sts remain.
Work 11 rows in stripe patt.
Now inc 1 st at each end of next and every following 8th row until there are 65 [69,73,77] sts. Continue in stripe patt until Back measures 34 [35,35,35] cm, ending with right side facing for next row.

Shape armholes by casting off 3 sts at beg of next 2 rows. Dec 1 st at each end of next and every alt row until 49 [51,53,55] sts remain.**
Work straight until Back measures 51 [53,54,55] cm, ending with right side facing for next row.

Divide for neck
Next row – K15 [16,16,17], turn and leave remaining sts on a spare needle.

Dec 1 st at neck edge on next and following 2 alt rows.
Work 2 rows ending with right side facing for next row.

Shape shoulder by casting off 6 [6,6,7] sts at beg of next row. Work 1 row.
Cast off remaining 6 [7,7,7] sts.

With right side facing, slip centre 19 [19,21,21] sts on to a length of yarn, rejoin appropriate colour yarn to remaining sts, K to end.
Finish to match first side, reversing shaping.

FRONT
Work as for Back from ** to **.
Work straight until 14 [14,16,16] rows less than Back have been worked to start of neck shaping, ending with right side facing for next row.

Divide for neck
Next row – K19 [20,20,21], turn and leave remaining sts on a spare needle.
Dec 1 st at neck edge on next and following 6 alt rows.
Work 8 [8,10,10] rows ending with right side facing for next row.

Shape shoulder by casting off 6 [6,6,7] sts at beg of next row.
Work 1 row.
Cast off remaining 6 [7,7,7] sts.
With right side facing, slip centre 11 [11,13,13] sts on to a length of yarn, rejoin appropriate colour yarn to remaining sts, K to end.
Finish to match first side, reversing shaping.

COLLAR

Join right shoulder seam.

With right side facing, No. 5 mm needles and A, knit up 20 [20,22,22] sts down left side of neck, K11 [11,13,13] sts from front, knit up 20 [20,22,22] sts up right side of neck to shoulder and 8 sts down right side of back, K19 [19,21,21] sts from back, then knit up 8 sts up left side of back. *86 [86,94,94] sts.*

1st row (wrong side) – K3 [3,3,3], M1; rep from * to last 2 [2,4,4] sts, K2 [2,4,4]. *114 [114,124,124] sts.*

2nd row – P2, * K2, P2; rep from * to last 0 [0,2,2] sts, K0 [0,2,2].

3rd row – P0 [0,2,2], K2, * P2, K2; rep from * to end.

Rep these 3 rows until collar measures 22 cm.

Cast off evenly in rib.

Join left shoulder seam and Collar.

ARMBANDS

With right side facing, No. 5 mm needles and A, knit up 70 [74,78,82] sts evenly round armhole.

K2 rows.

Cast off.

TO MAKE UP

Do not press. Join side seams.

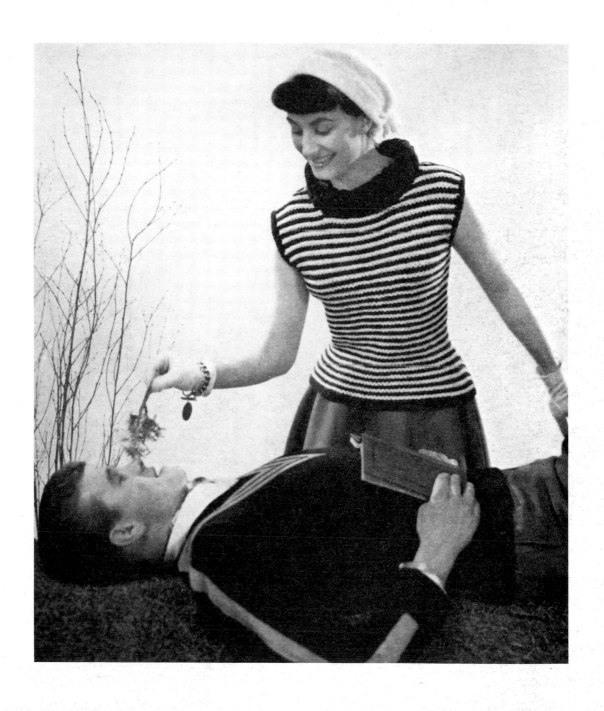

Yarn Equivalents for the UK, South Africa, Hong Kong, New Zealand, Canada, Australia and the USA

Most of the yarns specified for UK knitters have alternatives in different countries, listed below. In the unlikely event of a yarn being unavailable from local retailers, the stockists given at the foot of the page will be able to help.

When using an alternative yarn check tension carefully before proceeding.

UK	South Africa	Hong Kong
4 Ply	Beehive 4 Ply Gemstone 4 Ply Superwash 4 Ply Young Generation 4 Ply	Purple Heather
Double Knitting (DK)	Beehive DK Gemstone DK Young Generation DK	Beehive DK Clansman DK Moorland DK Patons DK
Promise	Promise	Beehive DK Clansman DK Moorland DK Patons DK
Cotton Top	Cotton Top	Cotton Top
Beehive Chunky	Beehive Chunky	Beehive Chunky Moorland Chunky
Cotton Perlé	Cotton Perlé	Cotton Perlé
Solo DK	*See* stockist below	Solo DK
Cotton Soft	Cotton Soft	Cotton Soft
Moorland DK	Beehive DK	Moorland DK

Stockists

Patons and Baldwins Ltd PO Box Darlington Co Durham DR1 1YQ	Patons and Baldwins (SA Pty) Ltd PO Box 33 Randfontein 1760 Transvaal	Textiles Department World Trade Centre PO Box 30748 Causeway Bay

New Zealand	Canada	Australia	USA
Bluebell	Lady Galt 4 Ply Beehive 4 Ply Fingering	Bluebell Patonyle	*See* stockist below
Herdwick Misti Totem	Beehive DK	Family 8 Ply Herdwick Misti Totem	Beehive DK
Brushed Caressa	Beehive DK Promise	Brushed Caressa	Beehive DK Promisc
Cotton Top	Cotton Top	Cotton Top	Cotton Top
Husky	Beehive Chunky	Family 12 Ply Husky Winter Wool	Beehive Chunky
Cotton Perlé	Cotton Perlé	Cotton Perlé	Cotton Perlé
Brushed Caressa	Solo DK	Promise	Solo
Cotton Perlé Herdwick Totem	Cotton Perlé Cotton Soft Pearl Twist	Cotton Perlé Stonewash Cotton	Cotton Perlé
	Moorland DK	Herdwick Totem	Moorland DK

Coats Paton (NZ) Ltd
Mohuia Crescent
PO Box 50–140
Elsdon
Porirua
Wellington

Patons and Baldwins
Canada Inc.
1001 Roselawn Avenue
Toronto
Ontario
Canada M6B 1B8

Coats Paton (Aust.) Ltd
PO Box 110
Ferntree Gully Road
Mount Waverley
Victoria

Susan Bates, Inc.
212 Middlesex Avenue
Chester
Connecticut 06412
USA

Knitting Needle Sizes

UK Metric	Former UK/Canadian	American	European Metric
$1\frac{3}{4}$ mm	15	–	–
2 mm	14	0	2
$2\frac{1}{4}$ mm	13	1	
$2\frac{3}{4}$ mm	12	2	$2\frac{1}{2}$
3 mm	11	–	3
$3\frac{1}{4}$ mm	10	3	
$3\frac{3}{4}$ mm	9	5	$3\frac{1}{2}$
4 mm	8	6	4
$4\frac{1}{2}$ mm	7	7	$4\frac{1}{2}$
5 mm	6	8	5
$5\frac{1}{2}$ mm	5	9	$5\frac{1}{2}$
6 mm	4	10	6
$6\frac{1}{2}$ mm	3	$10\frac{1}{2}$	$6\frac{1}{2}$
7 mm	2	–	7
$7\frac{1}{2}$ mm	1	–	$7\frac{1}{2}$
8 mm	0	11	8
9 mm	00	13	9
10 mm	000	15	10

Credits

Photographs: Jill Furmanovsky Associates;
Stylist: Jane Ripley;
Make-up created by Karen Mortlock using Max Factor
Classic range;
Hair by Heidi at Smile, King's Road, Chelsea, London;
Additional garments, apart from those belonging to the
models, kindly supplied by Levi Strauss from their summer
1985 range;
Hats, apart from hand-knitted items, kindly loaned by The
Hat Shop, Neal Street, Covent Garden, London, WC2;
Rennie chair from a selection at Liberty, London;
Cane chairs from a selection at Art Deco to the Fifties, Cross
Street, Islington, London;
Art Nouveau plant stand from Galerie 1900, Camden High
Street, London.